IF JESUS COULD NOT SAVE HIMSELF, HOW WOULD HE SAVE ME?

A California Mexican in an Anglo Midwestern Protestant Faith

Julian Segura Camacho

Hamilton Books
A member of
The Rowman & Littlefield Publishing Group
Lanham · Boulder · New York · Toronto · Plymouth, UK

Library of Congress Control Number: 2012934898
ISBN: 978-0-7618-5883-6 (paperback : alk. paper)
eISBN: 978-0-7618-5884-3

Cover image by Julian Segura Camacho

Dedication:
Ken Hillman Sr. & Fernando Hillman:
You are never forgotten!

Ken and Linda Hillman
John, Nancy and Jan Hillman

To the intersection of Oceangate Blvd & 95th Street:
My Outside Church

Scott Moseley: we re-found each other after 20 years

Quote from my father in law

"Why would I want to be saved, I was born saved as a Catholic.
Why would I want to become a born again Christian, those churches are made
up of losers: they are all recovering drug addicts, recovering criminals, recov-
ering whores.
Do you really want to be associated to people like that, I was born saved."

Theodorus Martinus Aartman
1940-2006
Born in Leiden, The Netherlands

Table of Contents

Preface

This book *If Jesus Could Not Save Himself, How Would He Save Me?* is a product of the 1980's when Southern California culture was not guided by artificiality or political correctness of today. Currently, people get offended by what others say even if it was not said to anybody directly. In the 1980's, people spoke their minds even if it inconvenienced others, as some spoke in racial terms both positive and negative visible in film or everyday conversation. Others verbalized in religious terms who believed that if not saved by asking Jesus Christ into their hearts—and they told you to your face—you were going to hell for eternity. People spoke their minds and it made for a better time because the populace could express their true feelings and did not hide hypocritically as they do today. This book even with the title attempts to capture that voice which pushed the limits even as offensive but is not without vacuum and stays true to the era where all people were equally guilty and simultaneously blameless. This book returns to that era of blunt honesty because this is how I was raised without academic interference or sugarcoating of a lived experience. As I once asked my childhood friend who's Black, Scott Mosely (he still attends an Assembly of God Church in Nevada) why were we accepted at the Anglo Protestant Church, he responded, "because we longed to those White people." Do not be offended by the wording, just enjoy the experience of Americans trying to be both religious and American in a time called Reaganomics.

Introduction

This book is not about bashing anyone's faith rather a search in comprehending an experience that began in a neighborhood in Inglewood, California next to the San Diego Freeway bordered by Century Blvd. to the south and Arbor Vitae to the north. It is a sacred place for many reasons: my first sense of childhood friends from the neighborhood, neighbors that took us in of different hues—Black, White, Mexican Americans, other Whites, other Mexican Americans.

Oceangate Avenue was also the street on which my father died of as a 30 year old young person of a heart aneurysm and where the search for some force or answer to life began for me. In these neighbors I took comfort and attached myself like a lost sheep and abandoned my own flock only to know that is where I always belonged.

From the friendship of the neighborhood, religious conversions took place that were extended to us neighborhood children with the sincere belief that we had to be saved from the devil's grasp and as someone who had recently experienced death unannounced their message of salvation seemed logical that also included feelings of not being left out and expanding the bond that I had with friends I considered family who were also White by societal standards.

Along went this brown kid who was made to feel part of this family to a White church in nearby Westchester and spent the next 6 and a half years learning about Protestant Christianity through bible studies, field trips, prayer sessions, Sunday church attendance, social congregations into their homes at a time these people were known as part of the moral majority. From these types of community churches arose Ronald Reagan as they countered the excesses of social and cultural liberalism and led me to experiences I otherwise would not have had. The issue of faith arose, I believe or tried to believe yet realized through my own experiences that someone was not there and in my maturity, independence and the lose of my special friend I removed myself to discover my own unpaved highway of life.

This is not a bashing of the conservative church as a whole but divulging the positive and negative experiences in a born again institution. The encounters eventually lead me to the path of self sacred independence and though I critique, this does not mean I do not value time spent there.

Chapter 1

South Inglewood, 1981

I.

It was early night. The sun had just descended and the night ascended in its roundness as I anxiously waited for my friend Fernando and his father who was suppose to pick me along with our friend Sammy. Sammy and Fernando had been neighbors across the street before I met them in late 1978. I had just moved into south Inglewood near Century Blvd. and the 405 Freeway. As had been customary to move every three years in west Inglewood, this move relocated us a mile and a half away from Manchester Blvd. and the 405 Freeway across from the famous architectural donut overlooking the San Diego Freeway north and probably leading to my diabetes.

Randy's Donuts afterall had been my breakfast mother in the prior two years. My mother had to help my grandfather Matiaz in Mexicali with his skin cancer treatment and my father had to work before the sun came up in those meaningless but meaningful jobs that never amounted to advancement but fed and paid the rent. Maybe that was the best it could be and it was. But as my father worried about taking care of his eldest son, he would buy my two glaze donut breakfasts with a carton of milk at Randy's Donuts and set it on the kitchen table. Breakfast awaited me.

But we moved and I never knew why south. Years later I saw a hotel replace the yellow triplex and came understand why we probably moved. Only in pictures does this place exist anymore. We lost contact with the neighbors Don Manuel and his wife La Coca who were Mexico City elites living a below average Mexican American life who clamored to live in El Pedregal area of Mexico City where they built a home. My grandfather and father called Don Manuel "El Maistro" which I understood later as the head of the block construction crew made up of worthless losers. El Maistro was the leader of the worthless loser drunks. Much like the White Joe plumber perspective of worthless non-thinking

1

mass of blubber and the White female lack of brains and logic, my grandfather Gus and father Julian avenged his Mexico City arrogance with this epitaph.

We also lost contact with Socorro the lady who would complain about how much noise my three brothers and I made but still baby sat us because the mid-1970's life required my mother to also provide. Though it would only get worse in the Reagan years. I was not quite sure if they were happy we moved and if my parents were happy we moved, but after we moved to 95th and Oceangate Street on occasions La Coca visited us in her Mexico City high heel wear and proper lingo and we at times visited Socorro in Westchester on Airport Blvd. and Arbor Vitae. Maybe we did like each other; I just did not comprehend it.

But now I belonged to a new part of Inglewood. The good item was that I did not change elementary schools. I would continue to attend Oak Street but would walk from the south north versus the north south.

II.

By now I adjusted to the new street but did not know how. Over time I became friends with Fernando and Sammy, then my friend Scott who was Black. Scott was Sammy's neighbor to the North. I would live half way up the block in a small modest but clean street. We had the poorest house because the roots of the tree in front of the house crouched against the walk way entrance had delivered us roots two feet high on a dirt feel. The front yard looked like a Tijuana house. But what could we do, it was better than living across Century Blvd. in Lennox where the apartments on Felton Street looked like vertical projects. At least on Oceangate Street, the whole street was clean and not slummy like the streets in Lennox. The eye sore on Oceangate Street were just our roots and our dirt patch, ok our house. The tree grew into the three step walkway breaking the cement and was almost inside the house if not for the cement forcing it up above the roof.

But we made do, inside the one bedroom home we had a nice and simple home that would become sacred and painful all at once. On Oceangate Street, the whole block was the playground. Because of walking, I made friends with Fernando, Sammy and Scott and they had nice grassy yards were we all played. By playing, we sort of became family. I went to all their homes and we generally played football outside or basketball on Fernando's drive way. We did not all attend the same school. Sammy and I attended Oak Street, Scott La Tijera Elementary in north Inglewood called Ladera Heights and Fernando attended St. John's Catholic School in north east Inglewood. Our unity was from playing in the neighborhood. Playing unified us even if artificially but through time we all developed a kind of bond because we all played on the street in between Sammys' and Fernando's corner homes. The corner attracted others from opposite ends of the street much like me. Scott's house was next door to Sammy's with a large yard.

But the two houses next door to Scott lived people who were related to Fernando either as Aunt Connie, the typical Mexican American name who was sister to Fernando's grandmother or another cousin of his mother. Her sons were a few years' younger but good friends with Scott. The older sister's played amongst themselves as their interest was not street football or basketball.

But Scott had an older brother Derek who at times would join us at Fernando's driveway to play basketball. I hated the sport, still do, but that brought the competitiveness out especially from Fernando's father who competed as a Laker and Derek was the real challenge for Ken who worked as an officer with the Los Angeles Police Department. We would make teams of three but Ken and Derek dominated the boards. Basketball is as much a Black sport as it is White and at that moment the culture played on.

The games were important because our identity was not defined by race. Scott and Derek were Blacks from Ohio, Sammy, Fernando and myself Mexican Americans, and Fernando's father Ken was White. I always assumed Fernando was White because of his last name but as young adults I learned that Ken was his stepfather but I always saw him as his father. Ken had adopted him as his son and did not treat him different from his own daughter Lisa. Lisa had black hair like Fernando so I just assumed both had the same father. Plus, Ken's family, Midwestern Kansans from Minnesota treated him as one of their own. The Hillman's loved Fernando and I saw it. And ironically Fernando, this Mexican American carried the last remnant of the name Hillman because there was no male heir.

Fernando's biological father had been somebody else who did not pay attention to him and Ken was the kind of father I longed to have. He provided a pleasant home even if Fernando's father was not his blood father, a private education, an affectionate father I longed for. My Apache father was too cold. But Julian Sr. was not wrong to be that way; he was just not that affectionate. But as a child I did not comprehend that. A Mexican American male must show strength and not show his weakness. In the adult world of work nobody is affectionate rather cut throat. Everybody is a devil. My father just prepared us early on.

Fernando lived a middle class life but then again, how middle class was he if he lived in Inglewood down the street from a house that had 2 feet high roots. But Inglewood was like this in the late 1970's. Mixed neighborhoods of Whites, Blacks and Mexicans who were united as kids playing in their country. This was an era where we kids in Inglewood played outside with each other. In 2010, children do not have this experience of the street as the playground. And fear did exist but we all kept an eye on each other. Grouping was a type of salvation we all found amongst one another and fortunately, the Hillman's never closed the doors to me or others.

Sammy also had a step father. As conversations always spring forth like a geyser, it turned out Rogelio was only father to Sammy's younger sister Yvonne. Sammy had a different father and his older sister Maribel had a different father. And both Sammy and Maribel were born in Tijuana, so they really weren't Mexican American. We won't get expelled from our country for committing a crime plus Mexican Americans are not born in Mexico. Whose father one was did not seem to matter but then again they came up. Scott's parents were divorced but his father figure was this Dutch man named Fred Van Hauten who was married to his aunt Donna who was Black. Aunt Donna would give Scott hell in a good way.

Maybe I was the fortunate one. My father was who my father said he was, my father. We were poor but that was not my father's fault that was our caste position for he always worked until the end in what ever job the system allowed him to do. Prostitutes are what we were without us wanting to be. Thank God for the food stamps we received. Another solution Sammy and Fernando's mother's had resorted to was finding another husband, much like looking for another job. It was a matter of desperateness and stupidity on the man's part, but it worked. Re-marriage got Fernando and Sammy's an equal proveer of income and the end result was a home. And yes the mother's worked, but their work would not have affavailable a home and to make sure, younger sister's came along to ensure the package. This sealed the deal, an 18 year commitment.

These were great male models in one way for they stepped up to support another man's sperm donation or a not so wise choice by their mother's. Even though I seemed to be the only one with a real father, my father had too married a woman who had a child from another man. In that case, Julian, Rogelio, and Kenny were the same. They took in women with a child. These men were great role models but later in life I could not do the same. They would support another woman's coitus. Both Kenny and my father were presented with one child but Rogelio adopted two and helped support them. We all had great role models from the men. Maybe too great to slop up the women's past. But that was their choice; we just played as development factored in.

The Reyes never closed the doors either but would want us playing in the garage or in the covered patio and the Moseley's always allowed me in to their home and use their backyard to play football. I learned to play football with Scott, Fernando and Sammy. Sammy was the competitive one while Fernando was the athletic one. I had no skill as I had no coordination and Scott was speed. My house was too small to have anybody over and even then when my mother had a fiesta Sammy, Fernando and Scott where there along with a few other people.

Fernando's family would invite me to dinner even when I invited myself over and never made me feel as a burden. Which I was! Weekend barbecues were common which is probably why I love tortas, hamburgers. At my home, we did not have a barbecue grill. Those dinners were important because as we talked we found out we had people in common. The first person was my tia Esther, my mother's aunt who they also knew because Fernando's mother, Linda Acevedo had been neighbors on Ballona Street in North Inglewood with the Venegas' who were my mother's cousins. Ken and Linda were shocked when I told them that my tia Esther was my great aunt. Linda had also been friends with a family called the Mares' whose mother Martha was my mother's friend and had kept an eye out for me as a child. Martha gave me my first crib and my mother continues to be friends with her. We were family. Thus the Acevedo's knew the

Mares' and the Venegas'. Inglewood was like a small rancho for me and this proved it and for generations. My mother remembered Linda as she was some years younger, Linda knew my mother's cousin Pedro and Pedro was friends with Martha Mares's son Michael.

III.

My parents became much more friends with Sammy's parents I think because they spoke Spanish. My father was Mexican American, had had a White stepfather named Clyde Childers but really shied away from speaking English. He probably did so because he was very selective of friends and was not one to go friend hunting. But my father was bilingual just as his brothers and sisters.

But with Sammy's family, I think the friendship developed because Sammy's older sister would need rides home from Inglewood High School after her evening program. Our location from Inglewood was not too far but for safety purposes a young woman walking home at 7pm was not prudent. My mother would pick up Maribel because Sammy's mother Isabel was always working. Then my mother became friends with Isabel's two other sister's who would come over and socialize loudly and pleasurably. I enjoyed staring at Malena who was short and gorgeous. She had a beautiful puta look.

Maribel had enough confidence that she would ask my mother if she would allow me to travel with her to downtown Los Angeles to go shopping at Newberry's on Broadway. My mother would drop us off on La Brea and we would take the 40 busline then known as the RTD (Rapid Transit District). Though others have stated it was the rough, tough and dirty bus, I never saw it that way. I looked forward to the adventure which was scary. I would sit and look around the strangers of Blacks and Browns but noticed that as soon as we left Inglewood, it became Black too Black for my liking. Then traveled to areas I had never seen before, to an island of homes full of strangers. At least in Inglewood, which ever part of town we traveled to, my parents always knew somebody in those streets.

We would eventually make it to La Broadway and I would marvel at the tall buildings. Maribel would state, "Don't get lost Julian," buy me my icee and shop her teenage savings away. I would have to help her carry her bags as I realized years later, I was pimped by my mother to protect and serve Maribel. But I was the one that needed protection. Sammy would not accompany his older sister and would laugh at me having gone along. I loved it!

And just as the Reyes's would confide in help with my mother, the Acevedo's did the same. Scott's neighbors where her cousins. Linda's cousin had a three year old son named Ronnie who was Black Mexican. They asked my mother if she would be interested in babysitting him. My mother for a year raised Ronnie who had curly hair and would follow my brothers as a little brother. My mother would frequently get asked if Ronnie was her son too. They wanted to know if that Black kid was hers and she would say yes, he is my son. The people really helped each other and this was one way. I remember my mother being sad when Ronnie stopped coming over. Once in a while she'll mention him. The fact I was able to play at Fernando's, Sammy's or Scott's house was a privilege and I knew I pestered them a lot. Sometimes I would show up without being invited or would want to attend their family reunions and they were receptive. Ironically, I would not be so receptive to a kid coming over like myself. The Hillman's were kind people. Today's society has changed and the distraught is ever present.

IV.

Then one day in 1980, we were all notified that the Hillman's were moving. Kenny sat Sammy and myself and began to explain that they would be moving to San Pedro and assured us that we would visit them because they were moving to a house that had a swimming pool and overlooked the ocean. And it did. I was shocked but assumed life was this way but realized that they would be around because the grandfather Ken Sr. lived two blocks over and Linda's parents lived one block north on the same street as the other cousins.

But I realized life would have a minor change and Fernando would now be gone. We helped them to move, rode in the back of the moving truck on the Harbor Freeway which cannot be done today and was in admiration at their new neighborhood. They moved into an area called South Shores with the house built on the edge of hill overlooking Catalina Island. It was a dream home, two story but built into the hill with the swimming pool. This would be a new beginning for them and a lose for us on 95th Street. But the place was far and I did not think that they would frequent as much because of the distance. Yet Kenny kept his word and weekend getaways were to be. For Sammy, I and even another kid named Ernest. We would all look forward to going and indirectly competed to go. When somebody else went, I would get jealous.

Then my father died and my world became distraught for its suddenness, for the pain it caused in my brother's, my mother, my grandparents Gus and Kika and everybody else. The night before my father had played pool with Sammy's father Rogelio, Lorenzo and Pancho who were Isabel's nephew and brother and I watched with security my dad enjoy his male time. The following night, he suffered the heart aneurysm and it was Isabel who I notified to call the paramedics. I ran in my pajamas to do so and she immediately called the fire department then drove over to the house and found my father dead on the bed. I remember her covering him with the sheets as my mother sat scared and bewildered with my youngest brother who was 14 months and my other brothers in the kitchen. Isabel was asked to do so much for a stranger and yet she did. Then Isabel's husband showed up but I had already ran around the corner to notify my uncle and his wife. As I stayed behind with her daughters, I remember the ambulance's siren and the red light piercing the dark living room. I got on my knees and prayed to no avail. As I would find out the next day, he had died and Isabel knew that which is why she covered the 30 year young man.

The following day I was notified by my father's younger brother that he had died. My tio Mike, just cried on my shoulder and as we walked around Sammy's house I remember him staring at me with great concern about my tragedy. I just cried.

The following night at my father's funeral, the Hillman's showed up at the Westchester funeral home on La Tijera. The Reyes' probably notified them, I never knew but they were there along with Sammy's parents and other old neighbors like El Maistro. I never forgot Kenny and Linda showing up in suit to attend my father's funeral all the way from San Pedro which was easily 30 miles. In all my distraught, he provided that emotional support. I don't remember my friends in attendance but Kenny's appearance was special and still is. My new life began and true to Kenny's word, they would invite us to their house for a birthday party or would pick us up for the weekend.

V.

Word was communicated that we would be attending Fernando's place for the weekend. My mother would give me permission to spend the weekend with them as along as I did not have baby-sitting duty. Excitedly Sammy and I waited as darkness sat in when he arrives in a Volkswagen station wagon. As soon as we got into the car, he turns around and begins talking to Sammy and I about being saved. It was important to be saved because Jesus Christ had died for us to be saved. If we were not saved and death arrived we could go to hell and not heaven. It was important that we accept Jesus Christ as our Lord and Savior and be saved. Did we want to be saved? Did I want to be saved? It was urgent I did so I would not go to hell for death was everywhere.

He looked straight into my eyes and I could see his concern. He believed Sammy and I had to be saved. I could not say no to a person whom I admired so much and saw as an adopted father. He had gone out of his way to continue taking us with them, had taken me on trips with them or family gatherings, plus his house, how could I say no? My trip might be in jeopardy. So I became saved.

"Lord, accept Julian into your kingdom to be saved and protect him from the evil of the devil."

"I Julian accept Jesus Christ as my lord and savior." I repeated these words after him and internally thought about my father if he was in hell because he had not been saved. Was my father in hell? But I could not defy a person I trusted because he had after all done so much for me. I was saved at the age of 12.

Chapter 2

My First Communion

I had been baptized a Catholic at St. John's Chrysostom in Inglewood. I don't remember but my pictures prove it. Then I do not remember attending missal until age 8.

My foolish 4th grade Cuban teacher Ms. Rivero had been a monja, a nun back in Cuba. She quietly approached my mother and asked us if we wanted to attend Catechism teachings at her mother's home on Inglewood Avenue, about a mile east from Oak Street Elementary. I think she competed with the White Jewish teachers who were pushing their "Oh Hannuahkah, Oh Hannuahkah come light the menorah" culture on us. She must have felt Catholicism was on the defense. It was but because of their own doing.

Catholicism took us for granted. They never attempted to be friendly nor really welcomed us. Nobody knew each other, everybody was a stranger. Attending mass felt more like attending a Dodger game. Not that my family was religious. Our religion was survival. My parents did not have time to waste praying to be saved from the harshness of the unemployment in the late 1970's. My father would use Sundays to rest from us by going to Hollywood Park with my grandfather. Horseracing was his religion and horses were the statues we worshipped. I'm not quite sure betting was a hope either. But to attend horse racing one had to make their pleasure from actually risking. It is like playing cards, a true player utilizes money even if they are quarters.

My mother would entertain us by taking us to the park or socializing with my aunt Lupe but frequent fighting kept us at distant at times. My mother did not really push religion either because we did not have any Catholic paraphernalia. No statues of any Middle Eastern figure. We barely had pictures of us hanging on the wall, much less would there be some Italian Roman soldier or a Palestinian of ancient time.

My family still practiced Cucapah Mayo Apache traditions. A belief in dreams, energy, the worship of death that she could appear at anytime, a love in food, cleansing and a broad interpretation of sex. The heavy focus relied on positive and negative energy and dreams. Dreams mattered quite profoundly because they had to have meanings otherwise we could not have dreamt them. But those were quiet practices not preached out. Catholicism was more of a social event but I don't remember attending any mass until the unwise Cuban teacher recruited me to partake in making my first communion.

Though religious discussions would come around at times for example when we visited my tia Rosa in a small one light town in Calipatria, north of Brawley in Imperial County. That aunt and her family were Jehovah's Witness and for some reason my father enjoyed engaging them in discussion. I was too tired, bored and young to comprehend anything. But the Castillo's were serious JW's. They would travel every year to Los Angeles to attend some large JW convention that I once attended. I could not comprehend anything and it drove me to desperation and restlessness for sitting 5 hours of ramble and ramble. But my parent's were not interested in attending any of their services. I worried that if we attended regularly, I would not get a present for my birthday or for Christmas. I know we practiced JW traditions of not celebrating our birthdays or gifting holidays but that was poverty not wanting to not celebrate Catholic traditions. I wanted my Christmas gift.

Then there was some older man with his green bible who would come to our house but stopped when my father asked him that he could not prove that God existed. I was happy because I could not handle sitting on the couch and staring at the television while it was turned off. That was hell.

I did have an Hallelujah experience in Mexicali but that was more for socializing. Every trip to visit the other grandparents meant that with my grandmother Alberta we would attend the Pentecostal Church out in the middle of nowhere near the Sierra Cucapah where Mother Nature provided Baja California with an actual show of who god is. The small church provided a time for singing, clapping and some sort of bible study. But it was not consistent. Here I was in Mexico and one would think that Catholicism was the norm but for me no, it was Pentecostalism.

Back in Inglewood, the Cuban teacher must have seen these White women push their Jewish teachings on to us and she did not like it. California after all was Catholic domain. There had not been a history of Protestantism much less Judaism. Though the funeral home where my father was held at in Westchester near Inglewood has been converted to a Jewish Church. But that is recent. One day a funeral home the next a church. But White Jews were new to Inglewood.

Ms. Rivero quietly approached my mother with her Cuban accent which I still don't like and asked her if she would permit me to attend first communion preparations. This lady might have been an ex nun but her vows remained in practice. 8 or 9 of us attended the six month long preparations and learned how to say "Padre nuestro" "Our father" in Spanish. All the prayers were learned in Spanish and by repetition. I did not know how to read in Spanish, barely could in English so reading was not going to be the way. Ms. Rivero repeated and repeated and I learned to say the prayers that way. She truly had been a nun.

She did not seem tired because she taught us with an extreme fervor, after having been our teacher for six hours. And quietly we remained. This was our best secret. I knew it was dangerous because to mix religion and teaching was not accepted unless they were Jewish teachings. Jewish teachings were permitted because even the vice principal Mr. Silverman was one. He later legally tangled with the Inglewood District for non-promotions and argued that because of his Jewish heritage he was held back. A White man suing a Black district for discrimination and claiming his religion as his defense.

Ms. Rivero was quite discreet and I suppose she learned this from living under the Castro Regime. If she only knew I would become a fan of his. In addition, I believe the Catholic Church in Inglewood approved the catechism teaching in Spanish because there were no Black or White kids invited. They focused on us Mexican Americans. And when we were done with the memorization, the script would now move to the mass. I asked Ken Hillman to be my godfather and he accepted and accompanied me.

How did the priests know about our preparations? One does not show up to mass and graduate instantly from the six months of teachings. The priests were in the cover up. Years later, I found out from another priest that the records of the first communion in Spanish could not be found because they were in a secret location. We had been the first group of kids in 1979 to have completed first communion indoctrination in Spanish. The priests were involved they played along to keep us from falling into a non state of religion or any other possible faith. We dressed up and took some pictures with the group and ironically a family picture which turned out to be the only family picture we have with my father. My first communion served a purpose for he died the next year. That is one of the few imageries of him at age 29. He died at 30.

Thus because of my guerrilla Catholic 3rd grade teacher, my mother began to take us to Sunday school at St. John but my father never attended. He would drop us off and then return but he never stayed or went in. He just drove away and was not like my uncle who would go and purchase donuts and coffee and socialize with the other Mexican men.

A good Catholic this place was, making sure they made money from the outside to the inside; from donuts to offerings. But the mass was too large, too many people and too much bass in the microphone. Catechism I liked because they were small classes but it felt more like school. The young White teacher would teach us about the Virgen de Guadalupe and assumed I would know who she was but I didn't. That was not my tradition; we were not from Central Catholic Mexico. I was from California where the rules did not make sense. I was taught about the virgin de Guadalupe from a White woman and our priests were White. And my first communion was conducted guerrilla style and incognito as a counter to the White Jewish teachers who were pushing us their Middle Eastern traditions from the US. But now I was a true Catholic with first communion and all but I could not say the prayers in English because I had learned them in Spanish.

On one of those Sundays that my father dropped us off at St. John's on my mother's birthday, May 4 th, he died and my prayers were not answered. No prayer could explain what occurred but Kenny and the Isabel showing concern meant something at a time all meaning had ended. My world got dark afterwards and at times I believe through dreams he said goodbye as I awoke crying.

We heard his voice, felt his presence and tried to survive the Social Security onslaught of why do you own two station wagons. I sought refuge playing outside.

Chapter 3

A New Religion and Church

When Kenny converted us, I went along because he had been there from before. He was not a stranger but because he lived in San Pedro, I would attend with his father Ken Sr. in a church located in Westchester. The name of the church was Westchester Assembly of God.

The first weekend of my conversion, I attended the new church with Fernando and his parents in Torrance, in the old part of the city near Torrance High School. The church was not their permanent home and they would rent the site from 7th Day Adventist who practiced their faith on Saturdays. The yellow building had nothing to do with the Sunday people, for they were not Adventist. But those that attended on Sundays all seemed to know each other along with the Hillmans. The preacher was a tall brusque brown hair male who looked more like a lineman with the Los Angeles Raiders. I'm not quite sure Jesus would have like to preach to those fiends. He was a serious believer but enjoyed the rock status. I looked at the White girls with lust and pleasure.

Though I did not find myself feeling out of place because I had already attended a Pentecostal Church on my trips to Mexicali out near the Sierra Cucapah. This was my version of Little Church on the Prairie on somebody's rancho. There were no elaborate décor or statues of Roman Soldiers or a blood dripping corpse hanging on a cross or men wearing Jesus robs that looked more like Darth Vader. I enjoyed the acoustic guitar and singing we did with the tambourine playing.

The church in Torrance was the same but with other strangers but I knew this was too far for me to attend with the Hillman's because it was too distant for them to pick me up. Plan B arose.

Apparently, conversion had sat in on all the Hillman's simultaneously. Not only had Fernando's family converted from Catholicism but so had his father and younger sister Jan. This was a big change in cultural life because they had been Catholics from the Plains states, Jan had attended St. Mary's Catholic High School for girls who then transferred to Bishop Montgomery in Torrance for her senior year. The switch came from too many Black students but not because they converting to another religion. And I would not blame Mr. Hillman for transferring his daughter to a more White school. Blacks were aggressive as I learned at Crozier Junior High School in 1981 and safety was needed. Even if middle class, Blacks could still be belligerent. I got suspended 3 times in my first year of junior high because I was involved into three fights. The racial animosity played out in rubber necking "you white girl comments."

My parents use to take us to Centinela Park for 4th of July fireworks or to play on Florence Avenue across from St. John's but stopped because it became too dangerous from the Black thugs who took over. My friend Scott would not want to go over either and he was Black. Race relations had a two way street. Many Mexican parents did not want their daughters to also attend Inglewood High School like my father's friend Carlos Coronado did with his daughter Mary (Spanish pronunciation). In a world of my rancho, when my father died and the novenario prayers (9 days of prayer after death) were recited, they were done so at Carlos and Evangelina's home in Inglewood on Olive and Eucalyptus. Mary was best friends with Jan from St. Mary's and I did not even know it until Mary mentioned it to me. I could not pray, so much for my Catholic indoctrination the year before, plus I could not handle kneeing on hard wood for 45 minutes. So Mary invited me into her room and I would watch television with her.

Inglewood was not just family but my country where many of us intersected. As Kenny wanted to make sure our salvation meant something, he told Sammy and me if we were interested in attending church with his father. He would pick us up on Sundays at 9am and we began to assist. Eventually Scott came along too.

Mr. Hillman Sr. was no stranger either. Because he lived two streets over on Felton Avenue, I had gone on occasions to his house with Fernando. We would walk. Mr. Hillman could be intimidating from the distance because he was very serious and as I later heard from Kenny, there were stories about Mr. Hillman not being a good guy. As a matter of fact he had been mean, a jerk, rude, disrespectful and an overall despicable person who was not really welcomed. He had left his wife Ruth but had custody of Jan as a teenager. He was a real person no different than anybody else but also a story that I learned from those Sunday rides to church with him. As he was responsible for his actions, somebody else had been mean to him. Everybody has their demons.

Mr. Hillman was born in Minnesota and raised in Kansas. He was a math whiz who earned a scholarship to the University of Kansas in mathematics until he was drafted as a pilot in 1943 for World War II. He came from a family of six or seven brothers and sisters who were scattered from Houston to Kansas City. He was attached to his mother but had had a father who was mean to him no different than what he had been to Kenny and maybe to Jan, to Nancy and to John the eldest brother. I believe the conversion to Protestantism might have originated from John who lived in a little town called Vernonia, Oregon, 40 miles north of Beaverton. Mr. Hillman's father had indirectly pushed him out in the 1930's by actions such as the time he interrupted his small garage sale. Mr. Hillman was in pain over that event into his 60's and when he moved out to

California and remained after the war he would bring his mother out to visit but not his father.

His father would complain but Mr. Hillman could not forgive him for the mistreatment and I suspect other painful moments existed. Mr. Hillman once drafted in his sophomore year in college was brought to Hemet where he trained to be a pilot. He became a B-17 bomber pilot and flew missions over North Africa and Germany. He was shot down four times and told me stories about shooting down German planes and killing German soldiers. He too had almost been killed and had to parachute out sometimes. I have a picture of one of his units. He would tell me stories but I was not a good listener but I really did not understand his stories. I did not have the language or the developmental capacity because I was still too young. I was only 12 when I started attending church with him. Certain adult conversations were out of my reach of comprehension.

Though I have always been amazed at his having survived four aerial downs at age 21 and 22, he was born in April of 1924. He was a hero. Later in the 1950's he worked as a car sales man in North Inglewood and served as a Reserve Officer for the Los Angeles or Inglewood Police Department. He would tell me he had a small plane and would sometimes fly on Sundays to San Francisco for an early dinner and fly back the same day. I always wondered why he never became a regular officer or worked as a pilot for an airline but he never returned to college because he got married and had children. Maybe confronting death so young gave him the desire to see his offspring and marriage provided that. Plus he earned good money in the 1950's that to give up a certain check seemed foolish to complete college or change professions. All his children attended private schools so he had a secure life in the 50's and 60's.

When I met Mr. Hillman he co-owned the duplex with his daughter Nancy but Reaganomics arrived and life changed for the poor. That was when I got to know him in his White Buick.

He would pick up Sammy, Scott and I and we began to attend Westchester Assembly of God. To the north west from where we lived. At first he was quiet and serious and would walk to the adult bible study and we kids went to the bible lesson for teenagers. My mother did not object because she knew he was Kenny's father. Sunday excursions became the real church for a friendship developed from the simple rides at 9am.

Chapter 4

Westchester Assembly of God

Westchester Assembly of God was a small non Catholic Christian Church of 130 plus people. It was located on Manchester Blvd. and Airport Blvd in between the San Diego Freeway and Sepulveda Blvd. The inside of the church was simple. No statues, just a cross behind the pulpit, a V shaped ceiling and pews on both sides with the aisle dividing the sermon space in two.

Westchester Assembly of God was a White Church. Most of the people were White but there were two Black families, a Cuban woman married to a Belgium and a Nicaraguan kid who lived across the street and no Mexican Americans. Now not all the Whites were American. The Belgium named Van Gerwen was a foreigner, and the associate pastor was a White Zimbabwean who had fought in the military against Black rule. There were German Americans visible by names and English Americans. Some were originally from Inglewood others from the Midwest. Some were hippie looking but bible carrying guys and others were poor, poor Whites from Kentucky. Many had too much money but most lived in Westchester with a few coming from El Segundo or Manhattan Beach. They had attended that church for many years. The poor Whites and the colored came from Inglewood.

The pastor was a career long minister who commissioned a salary from many of these families and lived in a modest apartment that the church owned. His name was Donald Trimmer and they all referred to each other as brother or sister. Most were Republicans and conservative when I began to attend on a regular basis.

This church believed in singing collectively, reading from the King James Version, listening to Pastor Trimmer and following the sermon from their bible. There were no Roman wearing robes or statues, no signs of the cross but they shared communion in the same way, had glass décor images of Christ on one side of the hall, baptized but at the moment one became saved on your own merit not your parents and collected money in the same way as the Catholics. I did not see the vast cultural differences Protestants and Catholics profess to have. And if they did have minor differences I never saw the differences different from not being related. The minister was a male and the priests were men. How different? The attire: a rob and a suit. Yes, the minister was married but not being married and having children were social conditions that some men I knew fell under.

The core of the ministry was in the ministry. The emphasis was in education. Bible study was vital but meeting these 14 year old White females made me want to continue if only to smell the aroma of them. When we arrived, we would go to the room for youth where we would have bible study very similar to my first communion instruction with the Nun Rivero. But the Catholics were based around learning the prayers though the Lord's Prayer but the Padre Nuestro was also recited by the Protestants but more as a reference.

The teacher's were enthusiastic and welcoming to me. The other kids my age were neutral but we became friends through time too. As they had been members, many of them knew each other for a long time. Spending Sundays and later Fridays for Youth Night became quite important components to their ministry. But Sunday mornings were for learning the Bible.

But I was confused from day one because it seemed more like a history lesson of the Middle East. But stating we had been saved was important. That meant we were protected with salvation. To be saved by asking Jesus Christ as your lord and savior into your heart was the central thesis to their faith.   And they believed it. This was different from my first communion teachings and the Pentecostal church I attended with my grandmother in Mexicali, Baja California. I did not remember any reference to specifically asking Jesus to save you. This was an urgent entry point even before the ministry because they had this fear that death could arrive at any moment and one had to be super prepared because if one died unexpectedly their eternal place could be hell.

In my 12 year old mind, I could comprehend this urgency because my father died so suddenly. Maybe they had some truth and as Ken Hillman reached out with such urgency how could I not wonder if what they stated was true. Not that I readily believed what they said but my thinking was confused because I was attempting to understand life and my life needed comprehension. I needed answers to the sudden deaths of my father and my mother's brother two years prior that rattled all of us. In simple answers, fate, life and death arrived as death and life arrive. But my thinking was not there and those White teenage girls were enough to keep me returning.

Chapter 5

Bible Class

When one was introduced you had to say when you were saved and why. Because the salvation was the key to admission, to make sure this was scripture they would pinpoint the verse in the New Testament that proved this was a requirement. I do not remember which verse it was because I have not opened a bible since those days in the early 1980's. But the rational was not different from the Catholics. The Catholics believed in the steps from infancy through the teenage years with the occasional confessions to the priest. That would protect one from hell but the mumbling and static of the priest and microphone was incomprehensible. The Protestants believed one confessed directly to God by praying and hoping someone listened. This ritual was quite vital in the services where one would put their face down where they were sitting and take the time to talk to their God. If anybody listened, it would be God.

In the bible class, after confessing that one was saved, they would spend time on the role of Jesus to behavior. They stressed following the rules of the bible from the Ten Commandments which are not just Christian or Jewish themes but good neighbor policy unless the wife of the neighbor wants to have sex with you. What is one to say? No! Some rules like thou shalt not kill are good unless someone wants to kill you or you join the army and are given orders to kill. Thou shalt not covet they neighbor's house, but what if my house was small, ugly, decrepit and dirty? Why can I not be jealous about their privilege? I only wanted the comforts that they had.

But I continued to attend because Mr. Hillman would always pick me up socially that I wanted his attention for me only. My mother would encourage me to attend and I hoped that Sammy would not want to go. Which he didn't for my selfishness? I wanted Mr. Hillman's attention because I felt I needed a father figure and all the goodies that went along. Was that a sin? I definitely felt guilty for wanting Sammy to stop attending and for him getting the attention from that 14 year old girl. I wanted that.

I also enjoyed attending bible class with Mr. Hillman because he would take me to eat with him afterwards at the Grinders or Denny's. Before my father dying, when he worked, going out to Jim's Charbroiled Hamburgers in north Inglewood was our Friday night outings. After he died, my mother could not afford to take my four brothers and me and as Mr. Hillman at times made eating out common, I continued to attend bible class because I might enjoy a patty melt. I felt guilty for that but this church at this time in my life was like a life jacket and to make up for my feeling guilty for using Mr. Hillman I attempted to be a good Christian. Mr. Hillman with his great heart would feed me. He turned out to be my Christian without him having to do so. He was my Jesus Christ in practice because Jesus never bought me a patty melt however Mr. Hillman did.

I took my new religion serious but all those rules confused me. No sex before marriage was preached but every time I saw a young female I was attracted to her, all I wanted to do was to have sex without knowing what sex was. Though I knew what attraction was.

No drinking and dancing. No drinking was not that common in my household though it should have been but my mother was preaching that if there was one tradition she detested from Mexicans was their worship of cerveza. Mexicans drink beer like water, the first thing they do is buy cerveza, they can't pay the rent because of cerveza and they love their bottle more than their children. I was scared of beer. Even though my grandfather Gus had been a Brandy drinker, those drinking years had previously ended before I was even born and my other grandfather Matiaz was the one who had taught my mother the evils of beer. Those worthless Mexicanos from the south were all too quick to spend their hard earned money on beer. Their consumption was why they never amounted to something. And he was right. The neighbor's husband in the next lot had drank so much that he had turned his existence into beer and beer had won out. How many men were not wasted? Yet the no drinking was different from being drunk but drinking is what leads to drunkenness. But I hadn't really been exposed to this sin yet. I did not have those cousins that perverted me with a drink.

Now dancing I had trouble with. Dancing was cultural but for them it was a sin. Somehow they used the scriptures to show that dancing was not part of Jesus' legacy. But it had been part of my legacy. Every trip to Mexicali always meant there would be one dance to attend. Dancing was part of parties, the highlight of Saturday night, communal, intergenerational and was criteria for future mating. The rule was that if you could dance well, the girls would follow. Women chose men by their dancing skills and for these people dancing were not permitted. This is where I noticed that at least in Catholic circles dancing and drinking were permitted. The mass and the party with beer and dancing went hand in hand but for the Protestants that was a taboo. I learned that prohibiting dancing was akin to bargaining for a lower price. These White Protestants would not do either. And bargaining for a lower price is something I am not good at. I am embarrassed to argue, maybe that was one of their traits that rubbed off on me. Now dancing I liked but I had two left legs so being removed was not that big of a lose until I attended my first high school dance and realized I was a bit rusty. The good part was that there were enough Whites that danced worse than me.

Other rules just seemed plain ridiculously that they did not want to answer. For example, there was consistent reference in the lectures and bible about sodomy. Now I had no ideal what that meant. When they would mention the rules one of the rules quickly mentioned was sodomy. I always wondered what that meant. I had no ideal of anal sex. I barely knew what a vagina was and wondered how I could convince a young woman to give me her vagina when I entered puberty and realized my nature belonged somewhere. That somewhere always drove me to any beautiful female. But the sodomy point was made subtlety and the other kids all pretended to know what it was. I waited and waited for months until I could not take it anymore when I asked, "What is sodomy." The Cuban woman Martha who was married to the Belgium man sputtered as she attempted to answer prudently but was in shock at my question. She quickly stated, "It is a sexual position not acceptable to the bible." I said, "oh okay," then wondered to myself what kind of sexual position is she talking about. It must be different than the frontal sex because they did not oppose that, they only stated that one should wait until they got married to have sex. But sodomy was different. And quickly moved to another discussion, but I believe I needed sexual education more than bible study and a woman to release my raging hormones.

And yes, homosexuals were criticized within the boundaries of the bible and their traditions but is it logical for two men to be engaging in human contact that requires lubrication. It is disgusting to me, unnatural and filthy but people should have the right to be themselves but this does not mean legislation should entitle them to property rights that males and females acquire when they marry. This turns out to be a property question, not a gay issue. If gays want to be gays, do it behind closed doors. Women, if pretty now that is a different story but most lesbians tend to be ugly anyways so they turn to other ugly women. Is touching really sex? So they critiqued gays hard but not with hate. They would state, "Jesus loves the homosexual but hates the act." Their near hatredness was harsher on Catholics versus gays. The gays they wanted to save much like a drug addict or a criminal but Catholicism they wanted to abolish. And if so, they should have abolished the gay clergy in my opinion. They have caused more damage hiding in a robe than some statue. A gay Republican has always confused me though.

Then there was discussion about Jews and how they had been persecuted by the Nazi's who needed to have their own homeland and were still persecuted. Besides the rules, bible study became a propaganda machine for Jews. I had been exposed to my Jewish teacher's songs but they were still White women to me.I had attended a Jewish camp the previous summer because our school counselor's friend felt compassion for me and sponsored my brother and me to a

Jewish camp for two weeks. It was another type of education with swimming, hiking, pillow fights and other activities. At first it seemed it was for problem kids but was really a combination of boys from not only Mexican or Black but for rich whites to working class. I had been disobedient that I almost got expelled. I was not really a trouble maker but just independent and curious. I did not like to be scolded and spoke back.

This was my first exposure to the horrors of war but the Jewish question seemed too foreign to me. But how could one challenge this blind support of a bible state where other people lived there. Their support of the Jews neared hatred towards Arabs who had not done what the Germans did to the Polish or German Jews. Even though this evil did not occur in the US or Western Hemisphere they proclaimed the urgency of protecting the Jews for the simple reason that Jesus was himself Jewish, really Hebreo which is different from being Jewish. Jews are Eastern Europeans from Poland to Russia and Jesus was not Polish, German or Eastern European. They heavily preached the protection of Jews as a continuation of the people of Jesus while in my Catholic teachings, Hebrews were not mentioned, Jesus was a Christian. They would refer to the Jews as the chosen people and the rest of us were the gentiles. Now that they did explain, that the gentiles were the non Jewish people and the Hebrews were special because they were God's special people. I sensed confusion about being special. Weren't we all people special for God? The answer was no, they were the special people and I did not like that. I resented that because it made me feel like a Mexican. Nobody made us special. The Whites had the better jobs and houses so they were special, the Blacks were being remedied for the wrongs of the past and they were being given opportunities, certain Mexicans were not poor and seemed saved to me, women were especially special and nothing about me was sacred. But I did not know their history at all which left me listening in limbo. Who wrote the bible that stated Hebrews were chosen people? Prophets who just happened to be Hebrews, Polish and German Jews were not part of this chosen group, only Middle Eastern people.

The bible turned out to be a limited history lesson about the Middle East. The bible had maps of Israel and the surrounding states, stories from those lands from Genesis to Psalm to Romans to John. There I could see that these chapters were from another continent with no relevancy to America. Just endless stories about Israel and I became confused that after a while, this was just the land of Jesus and these chapters provided examples that Jesus was the Messiah. He was the chosen one and was traceable from David to Solomon to the New Testament. Maybe David impregnated the married wife whose husband was sent to the front line by King David to be killed. Maybe that is where the Jesus line came from or was it the murdered husband who had conceived before he left. But Jews were special because they were Jesus' people and we were gentiles. I could not quite believe that logic along with other stories.

Walking on water was one of those myths I could not believe even if they paid me. Nobody walks on water except when the whales or dolphins come up for water. But that story was told over and over again that I listened without question because the others listened with their mouth open and ate the fly of an unrealistic story that was at best a good lie. But my mind could not question nor challenge for they believed the story to be true. The basis of belief was in these miracles. A human walking on water? Jesus probably did not even know how to swim. But this was a story that had been told over and over again that it became real because of its voiced repetition. A human flying a plane from one continent to another is a miracle. How many miracles could there exist 2000 years ago?

Another mad miracle was turning water into wine. The story was told that the power of Jesus was so great that he turned water into wine to prove his divinity. And I listened in carefully without question. The Cuban teacher Martha was excited as she professed his ability to make Cherry flavored Kool-Aid. In a rational world, a person would know that the conversion of water into wine is impossible instantly. First the grapes are needed and there was no mention of grapes. Second, wine making is based on fermentation and that takes a long time. It seemed that they violated one of those laws which was to not tell a lie and that was what they did and us teenagers believed their chicanery with a happy smile. But I continued to attend and listened to more pro Jewish comments with no reference to others that lived in the area they called Palestine. It was almost if these other natives had no place simply because they were not Hebrews. Jesus became a first person, a 2000 year old person who loved you. And they would say it with compassion that to turn someone away because they were too kind seemed wrong even with all those mythical stories that were lies which became truths. Jesus loves you.

Another vital lesson was the rapture. The rapture was a central component to their belief system because they vehemently believed that the second coming of Christ was imminent and it could happen at anytime. They quoted a scripture which I do not remember nor care to but the rapture was like science fiction in the bible. The science fiction which they predated could occur within the late 1980's as Mr. Hillman told me. He predicted that the rapture could hit in his life time. It was possible. When the rapture hit, those saved would ascend and meet Jesus in the sky. Those who died but saved would arise along with the livings that were saved. When the logical question arose of "what will happen to those that are driving their vehicles," the cars will continue to move and most likely crash. I just imagined the chaos spread all over Los Angeles with some vehicles driving themselves and spinning out of control. What about those not saved? The rapture arrived and took them to meet Jesus and those not saved were left behind. It was eerily but kind of Old Testamental. More like Sadam and Gamorrah being destroyed for their paganism and support of the fleshly activities.

Mr. Hillman was serious about the rapture and its nearness but I could not challenge him because that would be disrespectful and my mother taught me to obey your elders, especially people like Mr. Hillman that want out of their ways to pick me up. So I just listened in bewilderment and confusion as I imagine seeing people rise up into the sky to meet the messiah. That would have been an incredible leap into the air with no wings nor rocket on the back. Just magic realism in scripture. So we all waited for the rapture. Still waiting.

These bible lessons had a point which was the basic teachings of their belief system. They believed our body was the temple of God and as such besides advocating for sex within marriage, they also forbade drinking and smoking. As I mentioned drunkenness as a valid public health point but drinking wine was even in the bible and they saw that as unacceptable. Their prohibition thinking was ever present along with smoking. Why would you inhale that smoke into your lungs? I could imagine alcohol and cigarette companies planning how to get rid of this section for it cut into their profit margins. In that aspect, Catholicism did not seem extreme, not that I understood the rumble mumble of the priest. But when I went to local baptismal parties, mass came first and drinking followed the whole night. Catholicism only required one to attend church before the party of drinking began. I believe even the priest would drink wine for communion as their words slurred but the Protestants would use a type of grape punch. At times the Catholics seemed more accepting while for the Protestants behavior modification is what they sold. Then their politics began.

Anti-communism was what they preached. We are fortunate to be in America because we can worship freely unlike those Communist countries where Christianity had to be practiced underground. Look at the Soviet Union. Christians cannot worship Jesus Christ freely. Their anti-communism sermon was extensive. Not that I knew what communism was. All I knew was that it was Russia and in Russia the practice of religion was banned. Their Christianity and anti-communism went hand in hand. The Communist countries were evil for denying the most basic worship of the lord Jesus Christ. Communism for them meant that they were persecuted. They felt the like the scriptural stories of Jesus being persecuted for wiping the Jewish leaders out of some temple or like Saul as he was being killed for spreading the new faith into Greece. Their anti communism was dogma and they not only referred to Russia but to Eastern Europe. The Iron Curtain was a place of no freedom. A free society required freedom of religion unless you practiced Peyote ceremonies that could not be practiced in the US. So they advocated for freedom of religion in lands across an ocean and spewed the same rhetoric coming from their anti-communist leader: Ronald Reagan.

I had no ideal what politics was at the age of 12 but one political figure I knew about was Ronald Reagan because of my father. When the Carter v. Reagan election was being dueled out, I remember my father gravely concerned about Reagan winning. He stated, "Jimmy Carter has to win." I could see my father in the 6:30pm news quite worried about White America's grandfather, but I had no understanding of why. I could sense this great fear based on a real past and later found out. Ronald Reagan had been the former governor of California when my father was a farmworker up and down the state in the 1960's and the "Gipper" was no friend to brown people like my father. America's greasy hair grandfather had been viscous to better wages for people like my father who was a high school drop out in El Centro and worked as child labor for America. From the age of 14 to 19, my father labored under hard harvests. Wages were low and the work was dirty. The unionization of farm workers was an attempt to increase wages and meet the needs of their family. My father wanted a future and Ronald Reagan openly opposed this struggle and insulted my father by questioning if anybody ever worked the fields. My father did and worried that Reagan's election would Californize America with low wages and inflation. Both occurred and my father died. Yet when Reagan was shot, my 6th grade class at Oak Street cheered that he had been hit. That was our political act because the meanness of Reagan was laying havoc on our Social Security cutbacks imposed by him. Reagan was Satan to me but at this church they cheered him and I squirmed every time they stated he was a man of goodness. I knew the truth in my home.

Ronald Reagan talked about anti-communist this and anti-communist, the evil empire but I always wondered what was communism. Their definition was strictly defined to not being permitted to practice Christianity freely. Other elements of communism were secondary. But freedom is what was locked in their eyes and even though the teacher Martha was Cuban, she didn't profess anti Fidel hatred because there was freedom of religion in Cuba. Catholicism and Santeria rituals could be practiced. But other elements of communism they were careful about, such as owning a home. In a communist country you could not own a home but even I knew that in capitalism Los Angeles, homeownership was not available to all. My father or mother was not able to own a home and they worked all their lives. I knew my mother could not afford a home which is why we lived in a one bedroom shack. One adult and five boys cramped into a one bedroom home and because the US was such a great country another adult slept in one of the beds because she contributed to paying the rent. America the great! Even people such as Mr. Hillman who had owned a duplex, worked all his life, fought in World War II could not afford a home. He was now renting an apartment with his daughter Jan. Is this how life repaid him? And I wondered what communism was as another lecture arose.

The Book of Revelations was also consistently mentioned because of the doomness in the future. Anti-communism inspired them to be martyrs but the book of revelations instilled fear of why they would continue to be a practicing Christian. The book of revelations would reveal a chaotic and hopeless future that was becoming visible and predictable. Revelations revealed to them what the bible warned them about. The bible spoke the truth. Their evidence was in the new economy where they feared the sign of the beast would be visible everywhere. They were terrified about a paperless economy because they believed in the near future everyone would have a number posted on their forehead like the sign of the beast. 666 was becoming visible because the paperless economy meant that some chip in our forehead would mean that we could be controlled. When I saw the Highway 666 in New Mexico I wondered if the anti-Christ would arise. The highway to hell returned me to Los Angeles.

Though they were not too insane because every employer my mother or father had were nearing that paperless money economy called slavery. It was already there. I saw it for I lived it. To not control their destiny was lead by Satan. Another fear they had were the predictions of the enlarged mosquito. The mosquito metaphor was a greater danger because in the language of the past the name for the mosquito did not exist. Their dilemma was attempting to translate what was meant by a mosquito. Then the pictures emerged of the mosquito which turned out to be an image of a modern military helicopter that looked like an overgrown science fiction mosquito. Martha held up the picture of the US helicopter which meant that the military was to be feared that turned out to be ironic because the man they idolized Ronald Reagan was doing everything possible to militarize the country more. I just sat there and listened, stared at the image and did not know what to think of the enlarged mosquito made of metal. It was too much to take in especially when they talked about the number one villain Ronald Reagan; I meant Satan, Lucifer, the devil, el Diablo, el chamuco. The Satan story was told quite frequently because the devil was stressed to be ever present as Jesus Christ was. Satan was all around us to lead us to temptation, to evil to eternal damnation. He would unsave us, he would lead us to kill, rob, have sex (though this I did not mind), and the devil would lead us to drugs and drinking. The devil was a bad dude all because he was jealous. If he had only been humble. According to the legend, Lucifer was the right hand man of God but no, he wanted to be in control. God had all his faith in him and Lucho took advantage of the power because he wanted to be like god. As Lucifer led the revolt, god defeated him and banned him from heaven. God then deposited Lucifer who now became Satan on the earth and he would forever lead us into temptation. The devil was ever present as the serpent that brought the human race into sin convincing Eve to bite the apple. It was the woman's fault for being weak but they could never prove were the garden of Eden was located. I thought the snake was a woman because they always were.

In every bible chapter, the sins were blamed on the devil whether Satan was present or not. The devil was even in comic type of magazines that always lead to Satan being the culprit. The always mentioning of Satan meant that he competed with Jesus Christ. If there was no Satan would Jesus even exist? Satan was something we carried until we were saved or you went to jail when everybody seems to become a born again. Satan led them there even though nobody had ever seen him. Satan would reappear later in the future as a friendly person who would con everybody into believing only to turn out to be the Anti-Christ. I thought I was the anti-Christ as I thought about that beautiful Christina who was the real reason why I looked forward to attending bible study. Just looking at her, smelling her, getting her to glance at me was enough for me to continue returning along with those patty melts that Mr. Hillman invited me to. After time I wanted to continue socializing with the youth and the young teenagers in their youth ministry so I began attending their activities on Friday evenings with Jan and a clearer understanding of the bible. With Satan ever present as I had heard from my mother that Satanaz once appeared to my tio Miguel, the bible seemed like a safety measure. Just in case Lucifer appeared and attempted to talk to me only. I always thought Satan appeared only to those people who were mean by nature like my tio Mike or Bill Taylor from that church. The name of my future band will be Lucifer.

Chapter 6

Youth Ministry

The youth ministry was something I longed to join. This is where all the young people socialized. Christ was brought to us through socialization. Grouping by age was very important because the faith developed according to ones age. And the youth ministry was seen as the future. I wanted to attend their Friday night beach outings and camping trips but I had to be a teenager and I was only 12. But fate helped me. Because I was tall, I looked like I was 15 but more important I was mature and serious. I took my bible serious. I wanted to belong.

My mother had raised me correct along with my father. My father was extremely strict. Disrespect was not to be accepted and becoming a dirty cholo would not be permitted. Cholos for my parents were dangerous, dirty, low lives that made Mexicans look filthy and criminal. Whether they were my cousins from Gardena or my uncle Ronnie and Sambo from El Centro, my father was not going to raise cabrones as he stated. My father's family was hooligan vulture like that would back stab their own family with no mercy.

Julian did not want that for us and consequently was really strict but distance was the best protector. Away from the low lives in Inglewood was the solution. Even in the part of Inglewood that we lived in did not have those neighborhood associations. The Cholos were in Lennox across Century Blvd. and in North Inglewood but not South Inglewood. We lived along the wall of the 405 freeway and there was no street graffiti. We played tennis against the wall. That strictness which I called care meant that I was a respectful kid who presented himself properly. And I wanted to please because my thinking was never to disappoint my mother. I had a profound respect for my mother who did not want to let her down. Plus I had four younger brothers who needed a role model. I knew that I was a second father even if I was not that attentive.

After Julian died, I knew I had to be a real father or at least a son that was not a trouble maker, plus I was scared to fight. I was not good at it so being a loner like was my safety measure. I enjoyed the fact that there were no cholos in that church. They still make us look bad.

But the major reason besides socializing and teaching involved in those fun activities was to avoid the secular world. Secularism was viewed as the world that we born again Christians should not belong to. Secularism was a temptation of the world that removed us from holy behavior. Yet secularism was more extensive than just playing. For them being secular involved music, film, avoiding the sins but only interacting with other born again Christians. They taught me to really stay away from those non born agains because they were not a positive influence. If there were misdeeds to be committed, their logic made sense but to not associate with someone with a different belief tugged at me. Most of the Mexican Americans I knew were not born agains but atheist followed by Catholics. Was I not to associate with my mother who encouraged me to go but who never attended? Yet the Christian world depended on the secular world because who would they attempt to convert. Catholics were the primary target of this church. There were no such people as others at this time.

However the thinking was not quite different from the few Catholic Mexicans I knew. My uncle's wife disagreed with me for attending that church. My friend Rafael whom knew of our attending would not come along because his mother disagreed with the teachings. How could one attend a church where the virgin Maria was not worshipped? And she was correct. They the teachers would mention that Mary was important but not one to be worshipped. I had no dogma role so I did not care but I found it ironic that the mother would not be important if she gave birth. My mother was sacred to me.

The secular world was unavoidable for teenagers of the early 1980's. Music was ever present with the arrival of New Wave from England, disco ever present with the most sexual song ever, "Lets get it on" and AC/DC. Dancing was every where. Figuring out if Boy George was really a boy was the topic of discussion for the girls. Richard Blade was hosting his video songs from the likes of Duran Duran, Haircut 100, The English Beat, Depeche Mode and Fine Young Cannibals. Though an attempt was made by keeping us together and introducing us to Christian music that slowly and slowly crept in but without me halting my interest in the music of the time.

A common event Friday night was to play volleyball and listen to contemporary Christian music. Which was not all that bad for at times it sounded like heavy rock or mellow ballads with a Jesus Christ message? But it was fun because the groups ranged in age from 13 to 18. There was a gender balance and the guys prowled the females like pimps as if they owned them. The White girls liked it; they knew each other and used this mechanism as a way of dating. The females were enough of a reason for me to attend. I had just begun junior high school and my body was full of raging hormones. I wanted to be out where the real world played but knew I was still young. I wanted to see females as my hormones asked for them and this church was the perfect fit. Maybe too perfect.

My literacy was also improving because I was learning a new vocabulary such as secular, sodomy, Jesus died for your sins, gentiles and abortion. Most of the time their discussions would provide a language instruction that came from the discussions as all fun was also built with a special mission. Sometimes I did not comprehend the wording but I pieced meal the discussion. I was conscious of not asking what did this mean or that because I did not want to feel stupid but also because I spoke another language. In my home, even though we were Mexican Americans, English was not spoken, Mexican American Spanish was hence I felt that judgment by these White people. Not in a negative way but in a different culture manner. Foreign to them even though this was the native tongue of the place they lived in even though they never learned it. And I did pronounce my words with my specific Mexicanism but I was not the only one who had an accent. The youth minister had one too because he was not American like me, he was a Zimbabwean who was White. However he had the accepted accent even if it was hard to understand with the face of an English man from the 19th century.

But Peter would drive the van on beach nights as we traveled to Playa del Rey and enjoyed the sunsets of the west. They really were great especially when Christina would go along and talk to me. I felt that as my first religious experience. My heart would pound harder and the wind blew her aroma into my face as she conversed about nothing. I was just happy she recognized me and talked to me which was why I would want to attend the activities. Notice young females and maybe a prayer would answer my hormones. We would make a circle, hold hands and Peter would thank Jesus for taking us to the beach.

Chapter 7

Royal Rangers

The Royal Rangers were an important component for the boys which I also began to attend. This was the Cub Scouts for the born again Christians that required us to wear khaki color shirts and pants. At times I felt I was going to work out in the agricultural fields but the Royal Rangers was part of the children's ministry were they taught us scouting techniques such as making knots or working on art projects.

They were held Wednesday evenings and were led by men who would also dress up. One of the leaders was a firefighter named Dave Sheets. His wife June Sheets would work with the girls on other projects but also sing and played the guitar. The activities were always begun with a prayer but quite rapidly delve into the arts and crafts with images of the cross or the dove. The dove was an important symbol because that represented the Holy Spirit which was part of the Trinity. The cross is a given, where Jesus Christ was posted at but the place from where he could not save himself. But the cross was universal in all Christian Churches with the occasional bloody body of Christ hanging. The more Mexican the church was, the more bloody it was.

The born agains did not use a corpse to demonstrate the pain and suffering so the cross was not as imposing. But the dove was ever present in a sutle way because the dove represented what Jesus Christ became after he died. So in our Royal Rangers classes we did many projects that reflected many images of the bible and varied on seasons. The projects I worked on are where I met Christ Sheets who was the son of Dave Sheets or other guys named Jon Herd, Eric Brooks, the Williams brothers: Mason and Mark along with a Nicaraguanse name John too. Here there was no distraction of females but just cub scout projects.

I was also able to bring my younger brothers for they had groupings based on ages and it worked because by bringing my brothers along their ministry was reaching out to others. And Mr. Hillman was always kind to pick us up while he went to the adult teachings. Which by now, I was spending three days at Westchester Assembly of God. But I liked it. The believing came from the fact that somebody was paying attention and willing to pick me up and take me home.

Later on, the Royal Rangers would turn into camping trips to Big Bear or Lake Arrowhead which became my annual vacations. We rode boats or played games and made me feel pleasure. There was fun in Christ. Though teachings were not pushed as heavy as Sunday bible class, the Royal Rangers provided that boy scout activities of the outdoor and arts and crafts. We ended the night by praying and went home.

Though one Royal Ranger activity stands out the most. Besides the "how to kill a rabbit when out in the wild" however, we were not taught to catch the rabbit; it was already done so. The hippy looking White man twisted the neck of the indefensible rabbit and we (group of 25 plus from different churches) all looked in amazement. Not all where happy about the rabbits neck being twisted and broken. I was given the fur I think because I was the tallest and stood stoically while the skin was peeled off. Later on the ride back Jeff Sheets who was the older brother to Chris Sheets was giving hell about the heinous killing of the rabbit while I carried the fur with me back to Inglewood.

It was disgusting, cruel but I felt no emotion. I swallowed my fear and stared as the neck cracked. "He could have been eaten but that did not happen," stated Jeff Sheets but I had been prepared to be detached because my grandmother in Baja California would kill the chickens by doing the same hand gesture. The neck would crack and the machete would sever the head from the body even while the body continued to jerk while the blood dripped. I sensed these Westchester boys had never seen how animals are slaughtered on the rancho because all their meats were bought in the refrigerator sections of the supermarkets. I was hold cold hearted but life had always been this way so I took the fur as a gift and wondered if this could be like a rabbit's foot on a key chain for good luck. I patted the soft fur for a long time.

But the real activity that stood out was a bicycle ride we took to San Diego. Dave Sheets asked us to get a ten speed if we did not have one. Somehow my mother was able to buy a used Schwinn from somebody. That bicycle was pretty worn out and rusted. Mr. Sheets was an avid cyclist and told us that he would fix our ten speeds and paint them. We were to train on our own because if anybody was interested, we would be taking a bike ride to San Diego. We would ride early in the morning for five or six hours and camp out in selected campsites along the beach. One of the adults would drive a van and prepare our meals and campsite.

I was excited because I generally moved around in my bicycle and on occasions had gone to the beach which was not too far but my bicycles were not gear driven. They had one gear and any slope could be hard on the body. But, I liked adventure and saw this as an opportunity to get away and have fun as a 13 year old. When I went to pick up my new ten speed from Dave Sheets, I was amazed at the transformation. The bicycle did not look junk yard anymore. It was shinning black. That man who lived on an acre lot on a private street near the slopes of Westchester facing north had a work place that was the envy of anybody besides the large white home they lived in. Sometimes God was just too good for certain people. But his kindness was shared even though there might have been some opulence. Many times I only wanted to go to their house to imagine I lived in a comfortable home.

The day finally arrived and we began to ride off with the usual 6 or 7 of us, including a Kentucky born hick named Ricky Smith who lived in Inglewood. Ricky was the thug of the group precisely because he was poor like my mother, but lived off of his Vietnam Veteran step father who was a Mexican American from Manhattan Beach. There was tension there but then again the Chicano married a white woman from Kentucky with 5 children of her own who looked like they were from the south. Ricky's facial features were southern, his accent and his poverty. He really looked different from the likes of the Sheets who had a better look to them. Once again, a man married a woman with children that were not his own. Plus Ricky attended Inglewood High School and was one of the few Whites that did so in the early 1980's. Because he did he learned to survive in a more aggressive tone along with another friend of his, a white guy called Crooked Head Roy. Not that it was dangerous because I walked all over west Inglewood but teenagers can be rough when race factors in and the southern White guy is the minority. He had no qualms about making differences between the materialistic Black values versus the materialistic White values. To me they seemed to be the same but he would revert to being White though he lived in a city that was equally White and Black and attended a high school more Black. The church people I noticed looked at his family different because of their dress and how they looked and spoke. They were too red-neck for their liking. They preferred the English bushman with his one foot long sideburns from Zimbabwe than those rednecks from Kentucky. The Smith's were too hillbillies for them.

But Dave Sheets went beyond that. He paid attention to kids and worked on our bikes. But with Ricky coming along who was two years older, the search for girls would be lead by him as we set off our rides with no bike helmets. They paid for the food, the camping supplies and the fees at the camp grounds.

We rode through Long Beach, along the bike path in Huntington Beach and stayed the night in Newport Dunes. We would eat rest up and began our hunt for women led by Ricky. Not that he was a slick talker, he just talked and we spent the evening with some girls from Van Nuys who did not hesitate to throw their bark at us. We sat around the campfire and got to know each other and later went to sleep because we had to get up early.

Then we rode the following morning and camped out in San Clemente at the state beach. We went body surfing and saw the school of dolphins who were amazed at our swimming. They would surf through the waves with such grace. I was sore and stiff but I had a mission on my mind which was to make it to San Diego.

Then we rode off past the Nixon Whitehouse and the San Onofre Nuclear Reactor and rode through San Diego where we once again camped out at the state beach at San Elijo. When we set off the following morning, I was shocked at the hill we had to climb. This is when the different gears were to kick in and it hurt but I would continue peddling because I challenged myself to make it to the top. However the hill seemed to keep growing and growing while my legs cramped until we reached the top. The reason I did not quit was because pushing my bike up hill would have been harder as the hill seemed to be eternal. At times I thought if heaven is this hard to climb up to, maybe I don't want to go. The hill became each person to their own as my blue Dodger cap inhaled my sweat, my legs burned with strained muscles and my asshole hurt from three days of riding.

But I made it to the summit which turned out to be UC San Diego. I did not make it first nor last but somewhere in between and that was all that counted to me as I saw the beautiful homes in that college neighborhood. No wonder people loved San Diego. I would too if I could live in those places. I knew the answer but this was a way that I was able to see life beyond my hole. Not that I had to go very far from Inglewood but it always seemed that only White people lived in those places.

We descended upon Mission Bay and floated like whales in the water only to quickly return to Westchester in a short drive. I thought to myself, three days of hard peddling only to complete a short drive, but a sense of accomplishment lingered in my having made the whole trip without pulling out. Though our mission revolved around Christian teachings at times I forgot we were engaging in Christ and learned to be a young man as my mother preferred me attending this church versus wondering the streets. Not that I was a trouble maker but my mother felt I was safe in those church activities. I rode home proudly of my feat.

Chapter 8

Prayer Groups

Tuesday nights became another source of bible teachings that were held at the Belgian Cubans home also in Westchester which was owned by the Sheets. Mr. Hillman would invite me and I never said no. They were social gatherings with a religious purpose with 10-15 people but for adults.

An opening prayer began the session followed by some bible phrases and their meanings but they turned out to be confessions of how God was good to people. This was 1982 when the Reagan Revolution was in full force. Life at home was hard. Our social security only went so far because my mother moved us out of the house where my father died. She had to. The house was haunted because my father's spirit lingered. Not that he was frightening us but how does one interact with a dead spirit who was in pain. I believe he reached out but it intimidated my brother Alberto and me. I always felt someone staring at me through the kitchen window.

My mother had always been aware this was taking place along with my tia Lupe who had also heard the voice. When the voice was heard by Alberto, my mother decided it was time to move. I never said anything about hearing his voice but I did not like being alone in the house because I could feel him staring at me. When I would check the kitchen window nobody was there but once I returned to the living room, I could feel his presence again. And it was not psychological; I saw his glare in the window.

My mother Monica was burdened by the dilemma of sleeping in the same bedroom where her husband had died. We all slept in the one bedroom house and his body aura was ever alive. So my mother moved us one block north, but this meant that a larger home would require more rent and my mother wanted to have at least a two bedroom home as we five sons grew. But it cost more as Reagan inflicted inflation and unemployment simultaneously. I could see the difference and the burden. Sometimes I wondered why we all did not die. I felt we lived just to suffer. I could see the American limitations in our refrigerator. Plus, my mother could not apply for food stamps because we received my father's social security pension that he had worked for. So we hungered.

Then my mother had gall stone surgery and we were left with a baby sitter. I hated it, hated it. My mother was stuck in Centinela hospital and we were staying with a stranger. And I was not nice. I was a straight mean vile devil like jerk. I let that lady know I did not want her there and her kids. She did her best but I was in pain as my mother could barely walk and I felt like an orphan. I rebelled and walked to the hospital to see my mother. Here was my last person who was really sick and part of me wanted tranquility plus regular food. I would open the refrigerator and it was empty.

Thus Mr. Hillman inviting me to the Tuesday night prayer groups was my escape again. Then people would begin to confess. Mr. Hillman was the first one. He would state from his Catholic life: "I was not a nice person. But I found the Lord Jesus Christ and he saved me. At times I deal with the challenges we face and he continues to be there for me even when I only have beans and rice to eat. He is there for me."

Then Marta the Cuban lady would reply:

"Ken, that is why we are here for to help each other out, even if we only have beans and rice. The Lord Jesus Christ will save us."

I use to think to myself, if Mr. Hillman is suffering this way, envision the Mexican Americans. Times were tough in 1982. At that moment I really felt fear because if this White man who was a World War II veteran, a Captain in the Air Force was living through hunger, imagine us. And I use to think at least Mr. Hillman was secure or at least better off than my mother but he was not. The man was living in pain and letting out his pride through these prayer sessions. I felt for him because I was growing fond of him and he was the person who would pay for my patty melts.

The others would pray out loud as part of the session was a one on one communication with the Lord Jesus Christ. They would close their eyes and raise one hand in the air and talk to the ceiling. I want along and participated and prayed. I wondered if someone listened and waited for a response. I just did not know what the response would be. The people's eyes cringed in anguish about meeting their lord and I quietly waited for the social part because that was the communalism to me. The discussions and laughter but the purpose was the prayer and teachings that glued the socialization because I'm not quite sure the friendship would have existed.

Others would confess of how they were lost as Catholics and missed the direct one on one connection with God. The worshipping of idols and statues was one reason they moved away from Catholicism along with other excuses of confession to a human. The scriptures made no mention of that hence why should they use intermediaries to talk to Jesus if Jesus could be reached directly through prayers. So prayers were enacted on but I kept thinking about Mr. Hillman's hunger and wondered if Jesus could take our hunger away because I was not seeing any conversion of bread into fish and fish into bread. Was anybody listening?

And we studied the bible more and more while some spoke in tongues believing they were connected to the Holy Spirit. The language of the Holy

Spirit was vitally important. It meant that there was a direct connection with God via the Holy Spirit and when they spoke in tongues it was God speaking through the Holy Spirit to humans. What could I believe? Truth or fiction. They were sounding off words in a language I did not comprehend but at the same time knew most of these people did not speak a second language (one spoke Cuban, the other Belgian but they weren't American). I spoke a second language as one of the few Spanish speaking Americans but I would have comprehended that language if it was related to Mexican American Spanish and it was not.

Speaking in tongues has to be understood as the climax of prayer where intense prayer sessions with their eyes closed looking up to the ceiling, closed tightly with one hand up and the other holding the King James Bible. I would pray, I believed as best as my 13 or 14 year old mind could. But I also would open my eyes and see what people were doing. How could I not? I was a nosy teenager trying to understand this cultural tradition of the faith. Hence the intensity of the prayer led to speaking in tongues and many sought to speak in the lord's language. When the unknown language sounded off loudly, the others quieted as a respect for listening. This was sacred times because it meant that the Holy Spirit was in our midst and even I comprehended that. I did not distrust nor disrespect because my mother had taught me to respect their religious traditions even if they seemed strange. But I had had Pentecostal experience from my Baja California grandmother however in Baja they did not practice speaking in tongues. Though they did share similarities in music, the acoustic guitar and the tambourine; no idols and they all referred to each other as hermano and hermana much like sister and brother. Hell, even the Blacks did the same but with a jive.

Speaking in tongues did feel strange but not enough to ignore it. It was part of the prayer rituals and prayer was what we were there for. After the intensity declined, we returned from our spiritual orgasm and socialized with snacks and went home to face the daily challenges of the Reagan Years which were beginning to weigh even on those White people. We were after all running from types of hunger.

Chapter 9

Sunday Services

Our midweek bible classes and entertaining activities would always culminate in the lecture hall for our Sunday Services. This was when the adults came together along with all the teenagers and we sat for the great lecture hall. This was why church really existed. To come and listen to the main speaker, a person that the church leadership hired to preach and run the day to day operations; he was paid a base salary which was not too extravagant and provided housing for him and his wife. They lived in a modest apartment that the church owned.

The pastor's name was Donald Trimmer and his wife who we all called Sister Trimmer. We always called Mr. Trimmer, Pastor Trimmer for he commanded respect much like priests are called father. I have a strange feeling about calling a stranger father simply because he wears a cloak. Father in my opinion is only reserved your father or your grandfathers only and nobody else. At least with the word Pastor, the meaning revolves around the metaphor of the caretaker of the sheep, he pastors over his flock and keeps the coyotes or lobos away.

Pastor Trimmer was a tall thin man with his Midwest look and swagger. And as such, most of the people at Westchester Assembly of God were migrants from the Midwest including my friend Mr. Hillman. In essence I was culturally exposed to this culture which can be both White and Black but most were Whites from Kansas or Arkansas. Now they were not the same. As Mr. Hillman originated not too far from Lawrence, Kansas others were from Arkansas, Kentucky or even Texas. Texas Whites stood out because of their accent and depending on the individuals they could be extremely conservative in their traditional gender roles besides the moral realm they believed in.

Pastor Trimmer had an oval shape head and had bald but never quite accepted he lost his hair. He let his side hair grow long and would then comb it across his from ear to ear. He looked funny but nobody made fun of him because it was disrespectful, plus he wore his head proudly that you couldn't make fun of him because he was proud of it. Much like gays are proud of being gay or Chicanos are proud of their ethnic identity, Pastor Trimmer was not apologetic about his natural wig. This was the last stand of a balding man who had not accepted he had aged. And many elders probably understood that.

Lastly, Pastor Trimmer had an incredible sense of humor who really knew how to turn it on when he had to, therefore his persona was greater than some hairdo covering up his baldness. Pastor Trimmer knew how to make people laugh and when he kicked humorism into gear everybody laughed. He was after all the preacher and lecturing is part entertainment and part educational. The intensity of the service was depended on how much he believed in the bible and he did.

Pastor Trimmer would lecture for about half an hour after, the singing, announcements and group prayers took place. I personally enjoyed the group singing because I liked to sing, but Pastor Trimmer sat behind the pulpit to the side in his suit ready to hit the stage much like a comedian or a musician was. He was serious, this is what he got paid for and he had to be prepared. I had once seen his cathedra study and saw the planning that went into preparing for the sermon much like professors sit and ponder ideas. He was going to hit the lecture and perform.

I could see his book markers as he used the bible to prove his point, his belief in salvation and why following the word of God was vital to securing that entrance into heaven. During those lectures is where I got to know America, Midwest White America in Mexican American California almost to the point that America was created from these types of lectures not from the Continental Army. The Bible was American as it was ancient as it was Middle Eastern without the Roman history shown in Catholicism. They wanted the bible in its perceived originality. They talked about this 2000 year plus stories as infinite, almost as if Jesus was sitting right next to them. It was part lived part believed and based only on those words as if those words were magically sacred. As if Jesus was an American too.

Pastor Trimmer would preach on many verses, but one of the major themes was to prove that Jesus Christ was the messiah by looking back into the Old Testament and proving the blood lineage. Jesus would come from David, the woman that might have been pregnant from another man, then Solomon that son with the questionable father and into Psalms and the New Testament. I honestly would get confused and start falling asleep because it was too hard to keep up. One verse proved the next verse in the next book and Jesus was the messiah, God's son came to save his flock.

Just as Roman Paganism was dismissed as valid Christianity so was Judaism because by proving that Jesus was the chosen one, they were in essence discrediting the basis of being Jewish. How can that religion exist if the messiah arrived? And for them to reject the New Testament was paramount to a type of blasphemy because the Jews were discrediting the nucleus of their Christian faith. They did not openly critique them because of the Jewish Propaganda machine of the Holocaust but by proving that Jesus Christ was the messiah they were in essence proving that Jews were flawed and cultish like. Yet the same could be said of the Jewish world thumbing their nose at the Christian faith for openly rejecting Jesus Christ as their chosen one. So the Christians believed God's Son arrived 1983 years ago and the Jews were still waiting for that messiah to arrive. Who was right or wrong depended on your intestinal instinct? Though once in a conversation years later with a Jewish man from Iowa, he stated to me that most Jews believed the Messiah occurred in the 7th century when Mohammed rose with Islam. Then the Jews realized that they were wrong but the new religion of Islam was created. Most of the converts must have either been Catholics or Jewish converts. Islam was not talked about and Jews kept waiting for the Messiah to arrive.

Pastor Trimmer was a serious preacher and when he got turned on, he would break out of that Midwest stoic culture and show some emotion by opening his arms like an eagle and proving he was correct. He would even sweat and the hair partially jumped up but remained in place as the winds of biblical emotions settled. His point was proven and the people applauded him with modesty but not the way Blacks do by jumping up and down in the movie theaters. Sister Trimmer would applaud her husband and the service prepared its end. Service after service was presented with the intended goal of saving people from damnation. So new saved people were announced during the first part of the service as they tabulated how many people would make it to heaven before they died.

But Pastor Trimmer was quite political. The political affiliation for most of them was The Republican Party as they openly stated in their service. This was the era of Ronald Reagan and the Bible Belters like this church were responsible for sending him to the White House. They preferred an activist religious president but based on this logic they should have voted for Jimmy Carter who was quite Christian like and had never been divorced like Ronald Reagan. Maybe Jimmy was too Southern for their likes but Reagan was not Southern nor really that Christian was he not known to be Church going, so how could he be a Christian if faith required schooling. And Sunday Services was about schooling. Plus the divorce irked them so they hypocritically kept quiet while simultaneously critiquing those who divorced as a sin of God. Yet being married to one woman for a life time seems strange indeed to having sex with only one woman is beyond comprehension.

Pastor Trimmer would openly state that God had his hand in the President of the United States. I don't believe my father would have agreed with him that Ronald Reagan was a God of man. Reagan was lead by God but from what I saw in cuts to Welfare and Social Security death benefits, I saw that he was lead more by the Devil. And the Devil I mean President Reagan flaunted cutting taxes and getting people off of Welfare as an act of God. I internalized being poor and looked at Welfare as a societal shame but realized that people needed that money. I bought into the social value that being poor was negative because most of those Whites especially the ones from Westchester were wealthy enough to fund the whole church, pay for the pastor and vice pastor's living expenses and pay their gangly dues to the head quarters. Those of us who came from Inglewood were the poor ones and we knew it.

Pastor Trimmer was this contradictory figure as he supported Evil Reagan but was friendly and cordial. Most Americans after all liked Reagan because he reminded them of their grandfather who seemed harmless with his brilliantine hair but deep inside was evil after 70 years of malevolence practice. I would rebuke the Reagan love because I was living the Reagan hate and could not forget how my father feared his arrival. Even my 6th grade class cheered when the assassination attempt took place as an indication that our parents were telling us this man was evil. I could see the homeless population increase instantly under Reagan and never forgot the angry Black lady working at the Social Security office tell me off aggressively, "those are the changes by the new president." I wanted to slap the bitch at that time for her classless behavior. At least under Jimmy Carter the cost of living had not been exponential but under Ronald Reagan we had inflation that was dealt with hunger.

People admitting they were on welfare and then got off of it as a miracle was seen as another act of salvation while at the same time ignoring that for one woman in particular, selling her body to marriage was her salvation. How is that not prostitution?

Julie was one of those showcases as she admitted to the church that she was raised on Welfare but had now overcome the sin of poverty. This Italian woman with her peroxide head was an indication of poor Mediterranean Europeans being a burden to the US. As she confessed she was raised on welfare the church, responded by stating, "ohhhhhhhhhhhhhhhhh" but she had been saved from poverty. She would now do her part to donate but donation from welfare recipients is like taking donations from a thief, you were judged for taking that money. Jesus had definitely helped her.

Pastor Trimmer also loved Reagan because he was anti-Communist and was calling those nations that prohibited the teachings of Christianity as the Evil Empire. Thus the country was lead by a righteous Christian, who was fighting the sins of welfare, communism and now counter culture. Fighting communism was part of the bible lectures though in the bible there is no mention of this system as good or bad but they made it biblical. For me it was not that important because I had no imagination until they would mention, "they don't have food in their stores" and the television images showing that the shelves in the Soviet Bloc were empty contributed to the fact that they were not lying. Though my thinking as a 14 year old led me to conclude that the shelves at the supermarkets were filled but my mother did not have enough money at times for those goods that it did not matter to me if the shelves were full, we could not buy them. And getting welfare was so shamed that buying them that way was just as embarrassing as heaving the refrigerator empty. My mother did not qualify for welfare because we received my father's social security pension but we could have used them. It would have saved major headaches. I was conflicted even as a teenager over comments like that but Mr. Hillman and I had developed a friendship and I used it to get out of the house but abandoned my brothers until I began to take them along and Mr. Hillman welcomed it.

Even at times Pastor Trimmer would give us rides home and would laugh at our ability to speak English and Spanish at the same time. It was contradictory but human I suppose. Maybe it was the Midwest in Pastor Trimmer and Mr. Hillman. Whereas California Whites by generation were not as receptive to us. I have seen this in Oklahoma were my brother lives and the White family he has married into. They might be Republicans but they did not oppose the marriage, maybe the second child 13 months after the first born-the phrase, "do you want to be a welfare mother" was stated but to see the German-Americans care for my Apache looking niece proves their love. Dailee looks adopted but that little girl is as Okie as them, whereas liberal Whites never really talked to us. A ride home meant something.

But Pastor Trimmer also had social causes to preach about. The evils of counter culture hippie drug culture. I missed the 1960's hippie Woodstock's, flower child dances and naked protests of San Francisco. That was my father and mother's era. But my father was a farmworker up and down California that he didn't have the luxury of drug consciousness. He was too poor. Now in Oakland, his cousins were Chicano versions of hippies, long hair with wife beaters and a bandana around their heads. They seemed more like Apaches which they were. But my father's older brother was a true marijuano but not by consciousness. He didn't have that luxury, he was a farmworker and used it to release his pain along with cerveza Coors, Budweiser or Tecate when in El Centro, the drunks beer by choice in the Imperial Valley. But he claimed failing the drug test from the Vietnam War draft was his life saver and who could argue with that. Marijuana saved his life for that moment. Sent home after three days.

Pastor Trimmer preached a type of American culture that was partially lost to the excesses of anti-American traditional culture but based on a type of logic that was detrimental to the health of a person. He preached that absorbing drug consumption was destroying the temple of God which was the body. This intentional harm had consequences because drug usage was filling a void missing in a person's life. The purpose was Jesus Christ and if they had this purpose they would not need hallucinogenic. Wasn't Hunter Thompson also looking for God in all those drug binges? Cocaine, heroin, and drinking was harmful to the body, marijuana was not so dangerous but they believed it lead to other drugs. They saw smoking more harmful. How many anti smoking organizations have not made the same comments or alcoholic groups not riled against the dangers of drinking or police agencies fighting to prevent DUI. I saw this logic because I had heard the same rational from my mother. Drinking is harmful because people spend their money endlessly; drugs are even more dangerous and could lead to death. That was not a positive view that people would want to see of you; all marihuano out. My mother did not use the temple of God argument, but the danger to the body was stressed because people who were drunk were ultimately useless. And she was correct. Even my grandfather preached the ills of drinking and hard work wasted away by giving to the coiffures of breweries. I can still remember his words, "those Mexicans are stupid for drinking their money away. No wonder they don't amount to anything."

The examples of drinkers or drug users in the family proved her theory and Pastor Trimmers preaching. What had the hippies amounted to? Dirty people. That was something I could not comprehend. How is not bathing counter culture? I have never been able to figure that out because I was raised to bathe everyday. Do people enjoy sitting next to people who do not hygiene? I have come across Irish or Russian immigrants and can not handle their body odor that reeked in disgust. Drugs and not bathing was not revolutionary in change rather misguided youth who felt that they did not have to abide by rules. Anti-war would have been a good stance but this hypocrisy is highlighted when the anti-war message arises after the draft is legislated in by President Johnson. Now that Whites were being drafted beyond poor people of color, they became anti-war. How is that not hypocrisy?

Hippies have always rubbed me the wrong way because after all their drug use, sexual exploration both hetero and homo, and not taking baths results in an identity crisis, the very crisis they were attempting to avoid to end up coming full circle back to Christianity as they aged. When all else has failed, they returned to the religion of their cultural birth and gave rise to the Reagan Revolution. With Reagan pointing their fingers at them with "I told you so." So 15 years earlier, they were hard core dirty people and now they were seeking salvation much like the prodigal child in the bible. That return made people like Pastor Trimmer prophet like. He was saying "I was right" without having to say so. All he had to do was repeat the story of hippies lacking God in their life and the hippies cut their hairs, repented their sex and cocaine stories and became new types of missionaries: born agains in the suburbs.

Pastor Trimmer was a cultural preacher because he preached for tradition those his tradition was quite young, Midwest 1950's but not the 1930's tradition because I'm not quite sure they wanted to talk about the depression. At times you could hear it was a painful era which is why they left to California where they could receive a different type of welfare in housing and employment and it worked. Now that economic success had had gone awry, too much economic freedom meant too much liberal freedom and that could not be reconciled because Jesus was not needed the way he was cried for in the 1930's. This type of preaching would not be of material hunger but one where material hunger had to be controlled because that led to the drugs, pre-marital sex and even turning their back on the faith. Pastor Trimmer preached to the older and mid age folks with a reassurance sermon but preached to the youth as to avoid what the counter cultures were doing. In Inglewood, there were a few of those hippie biker rider White gangs and once at the wedding of a Kentucky born White teenager who married at 18, those White biker people were embarrassing in their sleeveless jean jacket, beer drinking and then bodily swarming festival they had.

Maybe the pastor was correct because my mother would not have approved of my hanging out with those kinds of people because she did her earnest to remove my brothers and me from the Camacho clan in the Imperial Valley. I remember seeing the youth pastors' wife Marta the Cuban lady in disgust as the bikers danced in their version of heaven which she described as hell. Hence many of those reached out to were the counter cultures now aging into their late 30's who needed a cultural cushion and admittance that they were wrong in their youth but without the chastisement.

Thus Pastor Trimmer was open to other issues of the day. And bringing guests ministers was a highlight of the sermons. There was an India English minister who showed up once a year to talk about the long shadows of evil or a Black gospel singer, even missionaries from the Caribbean or South America. The missionaries brought their stories, images of what they did, who was saved, and the importance of establishing schools and lunch programs. They did ask for money but that was part of the tithing which was no different than forced union dues. At least in tithing you did so happily versus in union dues, you always felt you were being shaken down because you did not have a choice. They took it out of your check. One missionary mentioned being in the Dominican Republic when the Johnson Administration invaded that country in 1965 and how they were caught in the swirl wind of a military invasion. They were able to get out but danger seemed to be part of the missionization. It was all for heaven.

But two guests that I have never forgotten was the scientist and the anti rock'n'roll preacher. Due to the fact that the church was against counter culture, the lasting legacy that remained was music. And because this was a majority White church, the music feared the most was Rock'n'Roll. For its anti-God stance, open sexual culture, overt drug usage and its sympathy to the devil. They abhorred bands that were critical of Christianity from Black Sabbath, ACDC, Ozzy Osbourne to the Eagles and even John Lennon. They particularly were repulsed by Led Zeppelin's "Stairway to Heaven" and the Rolling Stones' "Sympathy to the Devil."

These sermons were specifically aimed at all the young teenagers who were coming of age and would bring in this preacher that traveled amongst the Assembly of God congregations throughout the US preaching the same sermon. The minister was not this goofy looking person rather a suit wearing White male in his late 40's. He had a message and it was simple: Roc'n'roll was devil music. And he proved his sermon by reciting the words of the song, reading them out loud and using quotes from the same musicians. They were telling the world that they loved the devil and hated Christianity.

The man whose name I don't remember quoted John Lennon's dislike of Christianity and his response was "looked what happened to him, he's dead." I was alarmed at the fact that he openly applauded the murder of John Lennon because my mother had taught me that killing was wrong. But he made it seem that it was acceptable because John Lennon openly attacked Christianity and under that assault murder was acceptable. It was disturbing as I continued to listen to why this was devil music.

Not that I liked John Lennox or the Beatles but the song "Imagined" made me think about no religion or no property, it isn't hard to do. Then to hear the near acceptance of legal murder made me question even if Lennon advocated the end of Christianity. Then the preacher would play music that had to be listened to backwards. He had taped the vinyl albums backward and he would pinpoint the wording from the sound. He stated he heard, "Satan, satan, satan" when Stairway to Heaven was being played. If you imagined you heard Satan, then you heard it but Satan always got a bad rap in my book, plus I liked that song. Stairway to Heaven was one of my favorite roc'n'roll songs that did not sound like roc'n'roll.

I also liked this music too because I had certain albums from my father's collection and I grew up liking roc'n'roll music. It was all around us. The late 1970's saw the rise of AC/DC and Rush. We kids back in the Inglewood neighborhood were listening to the radio station KLOS 95.5 and were fascinated by the guitar sounds. Did we listen to the words? We tried to with our best limited literary imagination. We liked it better than the Black soul music with the high pitch sounds until Rick James came out with "Superfreak" but I also liked disco. Who didn't?

Then after bashing Led Zeppelin's Stairway to Hell, because hell was in the west as the song mentioned, he moved on to AC/DC. His sermon was easily proved because he just recited the song "Highway to Hell" and the horns sticking out of one of the musicians head. These guys openly accepted the devil and in the bible, the devil is public enemy number 1. But I liked that song "Highway to Hell," still do, life feels like hell sometimes. Every workplace has been hell. All my bosses and all of my former co-workers have been hell and worse than the devil. The Reagan Years at times felt like hell. Hell was all around us, we lived in hell.

Blue Oyster Cult was singled out for their song "Don't fear the Reaper." The song was evil because it was about suicide and suicide was a sin. I particularly loved that song with its melody and the phrases, "Romeo and Juliet, are together in eternity, 40,000 men and women everyday are in eternity, don't fear the reaper." Death was feared in his world. He was probably a Christian because he feared dying whereas I at times wondered about death if it was as bad as they made it seem. Suicidal thoughts creped in especially when I was hungry and felt hopeless, maybe death would be better but I purely liked the music. He just explained the song more thoroughly.

Then he critiqued a song that I really did not like but had been played so much you somewhat liked it, *Hotel California*. Now I was an Eagles fan because they sounded like Mexican Ranchera music in English. He first began by playing the song backwards and claiming he heard the word *Lucifer*. I heard something not comprehensible but he heard Lucifer. Then he would show an image of inside the album and pointed that upstairs was a man named Alistair Crowley who was head of the church of the devil. A man would be seen there but if he knew who he was, I guess he was correct. Then he stated, listen to the word, *"On a dark desert highway, you may check out but never leave."* But I never understood that phrase to mean hell. Was California hell? At times it felt like hell and other times it felt like the promise land but I always believe it depended on the neighborhood your mother or father could afford. The more into east Inglewood you went the more hell appeared. And when I traveled to the Imperial Valley in the summer, that was hell, literally hell, the land burned there.

But I continued liking The Eagles but at times wondered if they were devil worshippers and then Ozzy Osbourne proved it. Ozzy added to his legend with the diabolical album cover and near defamation of the cross which was sacrosanct to the Christians. Then there was this myth about his biting off some bird head which I never knew if it was real or not. In these days there was no such thing as the gossip net. If it was recited from one mouth to the other it must have been true. In those days once gossip became fact there was no way of breaking the stigmatism of the person. And Ozzy was a freak on drugs who added to his legend. Ozzy looked like he needed Jesus, he needed to be saved, his drug usage proved it. And Ozzy was a tortured soul as his famous song "Crazy Train" indicated. Life is like a train out of control that takes you along whether you want to go on or not. But the metaphor of pain was ignored because diabolical imagery was used. I was not an Ozzy fan but many were and his influence was feared. Ozzy sang a better tune than Jesus though.

I noticed that this was something associated with the world of Roc'n'Roll in English because in Spanish there were no concerns about the devil. Not that I listened too much but they were always about love and romance and heartache which was different from the world in English. And the minister returned almost once a year as if to keep the message going. After the third time, a White washed Nicaraguan woman who lived in El Segundo stated the following as the same message played on about devil music: *"Thank god, I like rap."* And we laughed quietly.

The last missionary visitor was the scientist who would contribute to Pastor Trimmer's contemporary ministry approach. This was new because the man was lecturing about science and the bible. We went from music to science and creation was a vital concern for them because there was a heavy emphasis on the Book of Genesis. The book of Genesis was their creation; there were no doubts that they had been created by the image of God. This was their science and disproving the counter argument was vital. The counter theory was Darwin's Evolution. Now prior to that event, I had never heard of Darwin or what he did. I had seen images of an ape to caveman to man but I never knew what that meant. But as the man began his lecture he was using overhead projectors to prove that evolution was wrong because the science did not prove the scripture. I saw letters that I remembered later from my classes in biology and chemistry. Most people were confused because the bible scientist was throwing too much information that was hard to comprehend. He stated that he had been an ardent Darwinist but the science did not back evolution and the bible backed creation. I was confused because I had no concept of where I came from other than my mother and father. Beyond that, I had no ideal other than my grandparents and beyond that I was not interested.

But I remember that many members of the church hated the fact that they could have evolved from the wild and that scared them because they did not want to know that they came from an ape. I felt that that was why they wanted the science minister to preach because it would reaffirm the notion that they were not related to the animal world because they were a product of God and God did not make humans identical to animals. I'm not sure what I understood or what I did not but all I can remember was that I left more confused than ever because I did not care to counter Darwin or believe in Adam and Eve. Plus, if we did originate from animals it was not such a bad thing because from my travels to the rancho in Baja California near the Cerro Prieto, the animals were not to be feared rather to be amongst of. They were part of our lives whether they protected us, gave us milk, eggs, turkey, honey, meat or pork they were part of our existence and that meant something.

Many of them would purchase stickers in the shape of a fish with the name Jesus inscripted inside as to prove that Darwin was myth while the myths of Chuy were real. How could the myths of Jesus hold more validity than the observation and study of the science world that Darwin looked at? Pastor Trimmer would exemplify those examples of miracles found in the bible as living evidence that Jesus was supernatural. Somehow, Jesus providing fish or making wine out of water was to be scientific and because it was written in the scriptures it was assumed to be fact. My favorite myth is the concept of the virgin. Somehow, the Holy Spirit came down from somewhere or appeared and impregnated her miraculously and because she was a virgin she was pure to have the messiah. For that era, science would prove that pregnancy could only occur through coitus. The penis would have to penetrate the vaginal and hope that conception would take place. If a woman was to tell me she was impregnated by a spirit I would not only call her a whore but a crazy lunatic whore. How could this be factually accepted and it was? Jesus' mother was psychotic and promiscuous. Even that I would entertain because pregnancy can be an enchantment sexually but the part I could not accept especially when thinking about Middle Eastern culture and my own Mexican American customs is the notion that a macho man of 2000 years ago would take the hand of a pregnant woman not his. I was raised to doubt that your child could be possibly not yours because a man can never trust a woman. Add the north eastern African traditions of still stoning a woman for infidelity or cutting off the clitoris of a woman for pre-marital sex and culturally it is impossible to view how a man of his era would take a woman with a child not his. In my family, my mother looks down on any of my brothers if we take a woman with children from another man. And she had a daughter from a previous relationship and my paternal grandmother has never accepted her for that, 50 years after it happened. In my lifetime, if a woman tells me she is a virgin, I'll tell her, *"yeah right."* As I was told twice by two different women, *"you penetrated all the way."* I just laughed and thought to myself, *"fucken putas, who are you kidding"* and told them "right! Darwin was Satan like but illogical myths were to be blindly accepted. Even at age 13, I thought, that must be wrong but continued attending because I had found a new home even if I had to believe in stories not logical.

Chapter 10

Riverside

Sometime in 1982 my mother conjured up the idea that a White flight was suited for us. We had rented a nice old house from the man David Sheets in Inglewood on Eucalyptus and Lime but my mother felt it was time to move to Riverside. It tore my heart. I would have to leave my childhood city, my Nino and Nina and my new adopted family.

This was now three years after my father died, she had met a Puerto Rican man and we moved with him to Riverside near the Tyler Mall. I was devastated and cried as the church had a going away party. I fought my mother about moving but she explained to me that she could not make enough to pay the bills and this person was going to help. I was told that every time I enjoyed the apple pie and oreo cookies was because of him. But I did not care. I was being torn from my newfound family and a stranger would replace my father.

We rented a home from my father's sister's boyfriend but we had to share the house. Again I hated the arrangement along with my mother and her new man who competed for attention with my brothers.

He learned after awhile he could not compete with 5 sons and the drive from Los Angeles to Riverside was killing him. I attempted to have a normal sense of belonging much like at Westchester Assembly of God. I believe I could make new church friends at another Assembly of God church. I found one on the directory, called the pastor and someone was sent the following Sunday. I felt I could then adjust if a new church would be open much like Westchester.

I was picked up and attended church with the White man in his early 30's. Sat through the service and longed to see Mr. Hillman and my familiarity. Other people greeted me and I felt like I could make it a go. I planned to go the following Sunday, called and was told I would be picked up. I got ready and waited and waited and waited. The person never showed and nobody attempted to get a hold of me again from that church. I stopped attending church and hung out with the local potheads in the neighborhood.

I spent most of my time depressed and walking up and down Magnolia Avenue. Max the dirty Puerto Rican eventually left, we associated with a cousin my mother had in Corona and then eventually we returned to Inglewood. Our salvation in Riverside became Antonio and Carmen Segura, my mother's cousin and his wife who were Mexican Americans. They had been our salvation and when we moved back, it was sad to see them go but I was blissful to return to my home and church. When I saw Mr. Hillman we hugged joyously. My mother had made a major mistake but at least she showed that she could admit error and rectify the horrible decision. My endless nightmare had finally ended. And there was no dirty Puerto Rican fucking my mother.

Chapter 11

Trouble

I returned to Westchester Assembly and returned to my routine. I reacquainted with my friends at the church, my friend Scott from the neighborhood but I attended school in Lennox. I picked Felton Intermediate because I did not want to return to Crozier Junior High in downtown Inglewood because I did not want to attend a majority Black school. The Blacks were too aggressive.

Not that Lennox was better because this was the Mexican Cholo capital of the airport area. But I was curious and it was closer except that I had to climb a wall that made the school directly south of my new home. We Inglewood Mexicans hated Lennox because it was a place similar to hell, maybe worse than hell. The devil had taste, he would not live in a dump.

I continued attending the church but after a few years as we teenagers aged I began to hear slight commentaries about being Mexican. It seemed humorous but that covert comment has double meaning. It seemed innocent to be picked on for being Mexican American but when the South African White minister in a discussion some of us teenagers were having about what nationality were we, stated to me that I was Mexican and not American with his inbreed look, impressed and depressed me. Pastor Trimmer and Mr. Hillman had never distinguished between us. But this foreigner did. He stated because my mother and father were born in Baja California, I was Mexican and not American like the other Whites. Forget about the fact that I was born in the US side of Mexico and my parents were still born in greater California. I was not American and at times that came out.

I was confused but it was not openly. But I hung out with some of the poor Whites and even one wealthy kid but it was the other circle of kids that indirectly let me know that I was different. Yet I did not care because that circle of friends Eric Brooks and Chris Sheets did not treat me different from those others I care not to mention. I just stayed away.

Then a massacre of Mexican Americans took place in San Diego where 24 people were murdered by some Ohio White man. At that moment I was scared. I could be at a McDonalds in Calexico on my visits to Mexicali and a hating White could come in and eliminate us. There were consequences to being

Mexican American and I was scared for a while but I continued to be involved in choir, plays and other activities. When Los Angeles was being stocked at night!

A man was breaking into people's homes and killing them. The whole region was on alert. One, 2, 4, 6 found strangled, all having the signs of an evil person. The Nightstalker is how he was labeled. Though his activities were not located in the South Bay nonetheless the ideal of a strangler was ever present especially because killings did take place by many Blacks. As it turned out there was a Black serial killer too out in the Westside who had never been caught in the late 1970's and the 1980's who was preying on older White women and even a Black female serial killer now called the Grim Sleeper.

But in 1985, the media reported an activity by local people in East Los Angeles that calmed all of Southern California. The media reported that some Eses as Cholos were called by Blacks had captured, beaten and held the Nightstalker until the police arrived. It was reported that the people who captured him were the local gang members that were on the verge of killing him had the police not arrived in time to save Richard Ramirez. When I attended my youth group that day, I remember the Eric Brooks and a few others come to me cheering the perceived cholos as having been community heroes. "The eses captured the Nightstalker, yeah, yeah, yeah." At that moment I felt a sense of pride because somebody like me had completed a civic duty even though the person captured was himself Mexican American. It did not matter because the cholos had done their duty with the pipe wrench but from a distance without knowing that he was captured by a man in his 50's and two brother's in the mid 20's who were not Cholos. Had that been reported a more accurate picture of the heroes had been regular Mexicans like me who lived their American lives without trouble.

From being murdered by a xenophobe White male to cholos capturing the Nightstalker, I could tell that being Mexican American in a White church would still have their limits. The racial humor bothered me because I was picked on for how I was born not because I was skinny, fat, big foot or had a bowl haircut but because Mexican meant something dirty. Now not all did that but it reflected that I was an outsider whereas when humored by Mexicans in the neighborhood it was because I was too tall for them or had not had a girlfriend yet. Even amongst them, humor depended on the cultural differences we had, Mexican American vs. Mexican immigrant. And with Mexican immigrants I felt the same as those Whites because I was not part of both of those cultures in the eyes of some.

But where I could tell that my race did not help me was with the White girls who were not country. The gorgeous Christina or Tricia would not pay attention nor would other females from retreats we took at camp sites. This might seem trivial or artificial but for me as a teenage male, the notion of being attractive to females was very important. If a good looking woman responds to me, she is telling me that I have looks for her. But the white chicks did not find me attractive even though they found other white guys palatable yet I was better looking. At least I had a natural tan with Black hair.

Though the notion of race would become explicit when the some what ugly female Tricia told me that her family was leaving the church. I inquired and she would evade the question that it was just time to leave. And did not move from that position until I sensed the racial conflict especially when I thought about where they lived: Manhattan Beach. That area was known as a White haven where few Mexicans ventured into. I afterall attended Hawthorne High School which was the buffer city from Lennox/Inglewood to Manhattan Beach and they did not like to elbow with Mexicans. And I say Mexicans because Black Inglewood would be too far because we brown people buffered El Segundo which was another White only haven. One must not forget that I would see signs that would say "Locals Only" and as I rode my bike towards the beach I could feel the tension. That was the culture Tricia's family came from.

Then on a retreat, I met a White female from Camarillo who half heartedly paid attention to me then moved away. While two other White guys, Mark Williams and Ricky Smith had two other females from Ontario in love with them. Mark was the son of that Italian woman and had the face of a sloth and Ricky was a long nose cracker guy from Kentucky. If there was someone out of place, he was it. Yet these women yearned for them but the female I met told me the following: "My father does not like Mexicans. He would not approve of this." And she repeated this enough times to know that I would not receive a goodbye kiss. And I did not, but these ugly crackers received love. Was I ugly? Not according to my mother and the end result was always a no. I would pray that Jesus would send Christina in my direction but he never answered and she ended up dating a White guy two years older.

But there were other issues also related to race as was highlighted by two Argentinean brothers who were still with their "che" accent in English. They were in their early 30's who were successful business men even with their limited English. What I admired from them was that they were not held by these non American issues. Whereas I was conscious about my English even though I had learned it equally with Spanish as a child from Inglewood, they mispronounced, had bowl haircuts and wore cut off joto fag tight jean shorts. But I was impressed by their confidence and they socialized with me. Julio Marin was one of them and at times I think he saw my cultural conflict especially when we would talk about how when I traveled to Baja California I had a positive experience with the youth but found myself in conflict with the White Westchester youth. He understood that and indirectly I began moving away especially when I entered my 10th grade school year and I participated in football and wrestling. Sometime later I heard that the Marins had differences with the church focus and they stopped attending and I never saw them again. I really liked Julio Marin even though I can't stand Argentineans. But there laid trouble beyond race.

I had befriended the family from Kentucky that lived in Inglewood. Their name was the Smiths and they looked like they were a cross between hillbillies, rednecks and crackers. But what they were was poor and they knew it. Poverty was not their fault either, they were born into it and escaped the moonshine hills and an abusive White father to end up with another abusive husband who was the Mexican American I talked about. I enjoyed the Smiths and their giggles but because I hung out with Ricky their son. The mother Lena after some time would explain to me the struggles that I might have been facing began explaining that they came from conditions very similar to Tijuana. They had lived in Kentucky much like Tijuana's poor lived. She would state: "We lived in cardboard shacks in Kentucky, I know that poverty." I was shocked because I never knew that about the US but was not surprised because when I traveled to Oklahoma saw towns with dirt roads no different than in Baja California. I'm not sure that trailer homes are better than adobe homes in Mexicali, when I moved around Los Angeles as I aged; I realized the likes of Watts, Compton, west and north Long Beach, Florence and Hoover, South Centro Los Angeles, Oakland, Athens and Lennox were places worse than what I had seen in Mexicali or Tijuana. Dust was not as dangerous as Blacks or Cholos wanting to rough one up. And I can't say that cholos were worse than Blacks because the cholos were territorial protectors; the Blacks from the rough areas saw other Blacks and Mexicans as those to be preyed upon. Maybe the Zimbabwean White was correct; certain Blacks could not be trusted.

Lena would further state she could sense dislike from those Westchester Whites from no other than Pastor Trimmer's wife, Sister Trimmer. Lena would state, "I can tell she does not like me even from the handshakes she gives." I could tell it bothered her and could see why. The Smiths dressed Kentucky with their polyester suits and laughed like Dolly Parton's father. There were others she would not mention but with Sister Trimmer that was enough as she represented the church leader. They also attended church in the church van which meant a social lowering when compared to the Westchester Whites. Jesse, the Mexican American husband had the sense to not attend probably because he did not believe in Christianity. The man worked as a gardener and was a Vietnam Veteran. He knew God did not exist.

Lena also had two daughters who could be movie characters but visible much more in the oldest who was short and obese. She was obese before it was an epidemic plus she liked Black guys from Inglewood and they liked her back. I could tell the eldest daughter had to deal with fat racism. And I call it racism because it was a dislike of a person because they were obese. The issue of obesity was such a factor that in the youth group, a Black guy in his late 20's by the name of James who was also a body builder gave a lecture on how glutton was prohibited in the bible. He quoted scripture and it was aimed at the two Smith females, the other sister Verlinda was heavy but also taller so you could not tell she was obese unlike her sister. I know I was also prejudicial because I would judge her as ugly because she was short and fat when personality wise, she was friendly, jovial and good spirited. There was no reason to be critical of her simply because she was obese; she had not done me wrong. Even then I knew it was wrong on my part. I was hypocritical like the others too because I looked down upon her for her look.

When James finished quoting the bible that over eating was a sin, the eldest Smith woman instantly responded. She stated, "I am offended by this lecture. I know this was directed at me but I don't over eat, this is a condition I have. This is a health problem I cannot overcome." James kept quiet with his muscular judged body because he stated what he wanted to say. The irony of the matter, a Black male critiquing a White woman because she was fat, even I knew that was wrong. That would be like picking on a brown person for being brown but I did think she was too fat. But I did not really care for James. I hated his Black arrogance and his confessing of sins in the open. He confessed he had gotten a female pregnant and she had an abortion. I'm not quite sure confessing gets one into heaven after a crime but James was thought of as a good person. I thought he was fake, who would then bring his drug recovering girlfriend who seemed she was going to snap.

But the Smiths had a brother who would serve as the catalyst of never ending nigger comments who was attempting to define what his Whiteness meant living in a Black and Mexican American community. He was poor and was from Kentucky which by White California terms was embarrassing. And he knew it but the females liked him. He would hook up with the White girls whether it was on a retreat or met Debby who started attending the church after some time away. Ricky would lash out his White comments about Black materiality which at times would get him in trouble. My friend Scott stated he used the word "nigger" on him but was called on it. Ricky though was a troubled young man who believed he could be a biker and a fighter at the same time but had at moments goodness to him. He was my friend but even with him I saw how the Whiteness helped him. At least females paid attention to him and that means something to a teenager. He went to church to socialize not to pray though at times he believed in being saved then returned to the streets of Inglewood.

Ricky and I would hang out with another guy named Eric Brooks who was a baseball player and I really liked him and his mother. On trips we hung out and played baseball. Eric was a guy who had a handsome posture and would attract the females because he was charming. His was from a divorced family who lived with his mother and his gay brother. The older gay brother kept to himself and did his own thing. His mother Betty was another of those Midwestern women who was friendly and receptive. They were also poor, she drove a pinto but she was not bothered by the material conditions. She opened her home to me.

Once, Eric and I went to play baseball and we hopped a fence in Westchester to get on to the field. We were having a good time when a car pulled up and seemed familiar. When all of a sudden, the man we knew from the church named Bill Taylor came storming out and yelling at us to leave. I was appalled because we knew the son of a bitch. His son Timothy was a few years younger and some of us had taken him as an older friend. I sat with the kid once at a Dodger game. Eric and I picked up our stuff and walked off while Bill the asshole pointed his finger to the gate. As we walked by the car, his son Timothy sat quietly in the car. We just walked by and called Bill Taylor every motherfucker imaginable. He knew who we were and treated us as strangers. The following Sunday I stared at him and he stared back but inside of me raged this anger of humiliation because it not only happened to me but to this other White teenager who were only playing baseball because we could not play catch on Airport Blvd. I knew to keep my distance from both of them, the son and his asshole father.

Then as I aged, I began to hear from Mr. Hillman's son Kenny and John that Pastor Trimmer was not all there. They felt he was at best a high school graduate with no theological training. They did not like the fact that we were still going to that church but Mr. Hillman would not hear of it. He continued to attend because he found a new family and enjoyed it. Yet Mr. Hillman had developed colon cancer and would find himself in great pain and was in and out of the VA hospital. The enjoyment I had from this church was beginning to fade out and as I turned 17, slowly stopped attending but not before certain events took place.

Chapter 12

By Your Own Hands

There was a woman, who was the wife of one of the church leaders. She always looked distraught and he had a calm demeanor with the look of Cousin Eddy from National Lampoon's Vacation.

I had heard complaints about him from Jan Hillman, Ken Hillman's daughter because she stated he did not believe that women were equal to men and he voiced that position. This appalled Jan and was a source of great concern about women's role in this church. The church on the one hand was a fundamental Christian church that did not have women as the pastor but they did not openly advocate rights to be denied to women. It was more that people had roles. The men had their roles and the women theirs with much independence. But obviously gender was a concerned.

The wife of this man who had three or four children seemed to be in great personal pain. Not that she ever told me or I knew about it because I never even knew where they lived but she seemed tormented. It was in her eyes. Her hair and face seemed distraught with her eyes watery. The woman carried a heavy burden that she could not handle any more. Then one day, word got out that she had taken a gun and shot herself in the bed. She could not handle the personal pain and sought death as her escape. We were told that Pastor Trimmer helped clean up the bloody sheets. The man moved with his children back to Kansas. In this case, Christ could not help her. Her death by her own hands had a profound impact on me and I always wondered what drove her to take her life and run out on her children. She abandoned her children when they most needed her and that I saw as a cruel action of selfishness but only she knew her struggles and as I sometimes wonder about suicide I remember back to her actions and think about the pain my children would go through if I took my own life with my individual hands.

Yet I sympathized with her because she had always been friendly and I valued that and greatly. I lived in a naïve world that people were generally friendly and not dangerous though I should was proceed with caution as my mother taught me. I had learned to distinguish between the streets or categories of people because their collectivity implied they were up to no good. Cholos in my mother's eyes were always seeking trouble, men in bars were placing themselves in imminent danger for alcohol was a great traitor and Hollywood Park was a place where the addiction to win was guaranteed to lose. Gambling only amounted to starvation for the week and my father never learned that lesson.

Westchester Assembly was unlike those places because from the outside world those kinds of people and vices never existed therefore the church was a societal protector from the evils of life. However this woman's pain could not be solved at the church and only by staring at the gun of a barrel could she find her answer. My mother might have second guessed us attending but the church was still safer than hanging out in a bar and associating with Cholos.

The widowed husband packed his belongings and returned to Kansas with his children never to be heard of again.

Chapter 13

The Deaths

Towards the end of my high school years, I frequented less the church because I played football and wrestled then I got a job as a supermarket clerk. I did not have enough time anymore for church activities as adulthood began to set in.

But when it came to certain youth events I attended. One of those excursions was camping to Castiac Lake. We were now either 17 or 18 and away from prayer and the bible we talked about women.

One of the guys whose name was Jon Herd had been dating a Puerto Rican woman who had also began to attend a few years before with her sister and her mother. The Puerto Ricans were a whole different race to my eyes. I did not have a positive view of them because I hated my mother's ex-boyfriend who was Puerto Rican and to be honest I found displeasure in their accents along with the Cubans. I just did not like that accent because I saw it to different to me. In addition, they looked part Black with some time of Caribbean native blood. I just found them too dissimilar. Mexican Americans and Puerto Ricans have zero in common because they are from the mid-Atlantic east of South America. Mexican Americans are from the desert only.

Jon Herd on the contrary found the older sister to his liking and she responded in kind. They dated. That evening in the tent as we talked Jon let it out that his father Bill, another evil Bill told him he could not date her because she was from a different race even though she was just as American as him. Jon was non chalant as he recited his scenario but made me remember when we were invited to their house to go swimming at their home in Westchester. I had this eerry feeling as I remembered his unwelcoming back in those days. For some reason, that was enough I could not take it anymore and stopped attending. I might have been hypocritical but I had grown and matured and realized I am adult and needed to fend for myself.

Then Mr. Hillman died which I knew it was going to happen because he had been fighting the cancer since 1984. Mr. Hillman's death devastated me simply because I lost my friend who had also become my adopted father. I always wondered why he was friendly to me. Was it because he wanted to make up the errors of his past or was motivated by the bible as his faith grew? All that I know was that he attended some of my football games, fed me countless patty melts and invited me to many Easter meals where I would see my friend his grandson and son Fernando and Kenny.

Mr. Hillman was the reason I attended that church. Here was the person who would talk to me, took me with him to Oregon and was even trying to show me how to play bridge. Then in March of 1987, he worsen, was hospitalized, suffered a stroke that paralyzed him and but could still acknowledge I was there with his friend Ralph. I turned away from him and just cried looking out on the windows. The following day, I was called and was informed by Ralph that Mr. Hillman had died.

I went to church and heard Pastor Trimmer announce that he had died. The church was consternated and at the funeral home in Inglewood, Pastor Trimmer gave his eulogy and that was why I respected him, because of his humanity. He might have been conservative on certain issues but much like he helped to clean up the blood of the suicide woman, he was there consoling everybody.

As Mr. Hillman's body was taken outside and into the hearse I cried endlessly. I was consoled by my mother and Dave Sheets, the Royal Ranger leader but cried that whole day and for a few days after. My friend had died who I truly loved.

Afterwards, I stopped attending Westchester Assembly of God. My brothers continued to attend when they notified me that Bill Herd had died and rejoiced in his passing. Soon after, even my brother's stopped attending. It was time to move on.

Chapter 14

2000

I had fled from the church after Mr. Hillman's passing but in reality, he was my church, my community, my Christ and the person who helped me at times. Once he died, my reason expired along. I cut off all ties to those people and only once did I see Chris Sheets and Jon Heard again. I never saw Eric Brooks or Ricky Smith again much less Pastor Trimmer. I attended college and rebelled at that cultural thinking because I felt the myths were too infactual to believe. Where I learned other myths that I should not have listened to.

I lost contact with the Hillmans but we knew of each other because my mother would visit with her friend Martha Mares in Hawthorne who would visit with Linda's mother Helen. I would hear of the Hillmans and my old friend Fernando who himself had separated from his father Ken Hillman and for drug use.

Unfortunately, in 2001, I went to visit them to the house they had moved to in San Pedro because Fernando had died. I never knew why but it was from a combination of drug use and the heart just giving out. It was hard to believe a person I had played with had perished and this unexpected reunion was taking place as I was a pall bearer along with Sammy whom I had not seen for years. The man died at 31.

There I was with Ken Hillman's other children, John, Nancy and Jan along with Kenny and had flash backs to the 1980's when I would visit with them. They were still religious and I was not and could not handle hearing Jesus loves me when I did not believe in that anymore nor did I not want to be rude. So I moved away again but still admire them and care for them in my own way.

Life later proved to me that there is no higher being and that I liked to sin especially with women but that does not mean I am a sinner. I just have a different cultural value on women and life. I can not believe in cultural practices from Africa/Middle East because I feel that I lose my own Apache culture. But on the other hand I cannot forget that there was much good and bad yet I somehow enjoyed my time there that ran its course. I cannot live with too many rules, I want absolute freedom.

I just believe if Jesus could not save himself, how would he save me? Lennox proved that he could not save me or my family. As I entered adulthood and the workplace, I realized I had entered hell, torture, anguish, misery, torment, agony, torture and a permanent living nightmare. The workplace is a permanent place of infernary with greed, backstabbing, chicanery, corruption, exploitation, a place of no trust and constant suspicion. I have found the fear of Cholos, gamblers and bars to be much safer, saner, and honest and much more compassionate than any employment I have had. So much for the educated lot for all they ever demonstrated is human characteristics only suitable for death role. I am quite positive hell would not want this lot because the devil would want honest villains and criminals.

Chapter 15

The Wedding

Pastor Trimmer's sermons were many and had an influence on my life that at times I remembered points heard in the future.

Twenty years later I was invited to a wedding at the Beverly Hills Hotel on Sunset Blvd. The wedding was the renewed vow ceremony for Ozzy Osbourne and his wife who had become famous for their reality television show. I could not believe where I was at on the New Year's Eve event. I am walking in and I come up upon Chris Rock before walking in to the event room.

We sit down and there are 200 people waiting for the ceremony to begin, faceless people I have no ideal who they are and I'm just an unknown face to them. The ceremony room is gorgeous with red rose petals decorating the floor where both Mr. and Mrs. Osborne are going to walk together. I could see the new wealth Carry McWilliams talked about in his book *Southern California: An Island on the Land*. Beverly Hills was new money yet in the world I was living in it was more money than I had ever seen, however these people were not Americans hence it was not even American money but the ceremony was taken place in the US not England.

And Ozzy looked like the drugs had wrecked him as he could not stop shaking. There was Ozzy shaking as he walked wearing his silver cross and thanking people for attending his wedding. He seemed different than the singer portrayed as devil worshipping and contradictory to the Christian views of him, he was renewing his vows of marriage after 25 years. In the Christian world that would make him saintly or at least it should have. With his fame and money Ozzy could have had his posse of rock bangers following him. He might have established his own form of Church or the fans at least could have the way Argentinos have with their futbol idol, Diego Armando Maradona. And Diego has violated quite a few Christian rules but he's a South American Native and they have different standards when it comes to women, marriage, children, a broader interpretation. And the occasional drug consumption is also a constant characteristic of Diego and he's still worshipped by women too. Now if Diego has his following one would think that Ozzy could too and have his own church and harem but he's been constant with his wife. Yet he likes his drugs but that is his life.

As I saw him go by shaking yet suited for his important ceremony, he seemed harmless and quite different from that fiend that he was portrayed as. I even met Marilyn Manson with his makeup and had a discussion with him about his interview and comments on the Michael Moore documentary "Bowling for Columbine." Marilyn Manson told me he didn't like the ending and the night continued and I even saw the Village People or their cover band perform "YMCA" and "In the Navy." Gay songs with the best beat. At times it was surreal especially when the only Brown people there were the servers and I was the lone guest.

Later that evening as I walked to the restrooms and was confused about the décor. The place looked like a fancy Mexican hacienda which it turned out to be. When my friend stated, "this was the hotel where the Eagles took pictures for the album Hotel California. They took pictures in the courtyard." I told her about the devil worship theory from my teenage church and she stated, "they were not devil worshippers, rather they were critiquing the worshipping of material goods which can be devilish. That was why they took pictures here. What better symbols of material worship can there exist than the Beverly Hills Hotel? If you buy into that you will never leave."

It was a good night.